Adult
Bible Study Series

By Thomas J. Doyle

Portions of the "Study" and "Apply" sections
were written by Carl C. Fickenscher II

"Catechism Connections" were written
by Arnold Schmidt

CONCORDIA PUBLISHING HOUSE · SAINT LOUIS

1   2   3   4   5   6   7   8   9   10   13   12   11   10   09   08   07   06   05   04

Contents

Leader Guide 115

Introduction

God promises to strengthen our life in Christ as we study His Word. The Our Life in Christ Bible Study series provides you resources to help you study God's Word. The series gives you an opportunity to study in-depth some familiar and, possibly, not-so-familiar biblical accounts.

Each of the 9 Bible study books has 13 sessions that are divided into 4 easy-to-use sections.

Gather—Section 1 of each session points participants to the key concept for the session.

Study—Section 2 explores a portion of Scripture through the use of a commentary and questions that help the participants study the text.

Apply—Section 3 of each session helps the participants apply to their lives both God's Law and Gospel revealed in the scriptural account.

Send—Section 4 of each session provides the participants with practical suggestions for taking the theme of the lesson out of the classroom and into the world.

Our Life in Christ is designed to assist both novice and expert Bible students with resources that will enable them to grow in their understanding of God's Word while strengthening their life in Christ.

As an added benefit, the sessions in the Our Life in Christ Adult Bible Study series follow the Scripture lessons taught in the Our Life in Christ Sunday school series. Parents will enjoy studying in-depth the Bible stories their children are studying in Sunday school. This will provide parents with opportunities to

- discuss God's Word together;
- extend lesson applications to everyday situations;
- pray together; and
- engage in family activities that grow out of the lesson truths.

We pray that as you study God's Word using the Our Life in Christ Adult Bible Study series, your life in Christ may be strengthened.

Adult Study Guide

World History	Dates	Biblical People
Neo-Sumerian	2000 B.C.	
Egypt, New Kingdom	1500 B.C.	
Philistine Invasion	1000 B.C.	
Assyrian Empire	785 B.C.	
Old Testament Ends	430 B.C.	
Romans	c. A.D. 30	Mary and Joseph John the Baptist Jesus Christ Samaritan Woman Man Born Blind

John Prepares the Way for Jesus

(Luke 1:57–80; Matthew 3:1–12)

Gather

Theme: The Warmup to the Main Event!

Key Point

Warning people to repent of their sins, John was preparing them for Jesus, who provides forgiveness and eternal life to repentant sinners.

Objectives

By the power of the Holy Spirit working through God's Word we will
1. describe the miraculous unfolding of God's plan of salvation through the birth and the ministry of John the Baptist;
2. summarize the Law and the Gospel contained in John's message;
3. explain how John was the warmup to the main event—Jesus;
4. express joy and peace as we anticipate Judgment Day, when Jesus will return to judge the living and the dead.

Opening

Pray David's prayer from 1 Chronicles 29:10–13:
"Praise be to You, O LORD, God of our father Israel, from everlasting to everlasting. Yours, O LORD, is the greatness and the power and the glory and the majesty and the splendor, for everything in heaven and earth is Yours. Yours, O LORD, is the kingdom; You are exalted as head over all. Wealth and honor come from You; You are the ruler of all things. In Your hands are strength and power to exalt and give strength to all. Now, our God, we give You thanks, and praise Your glorious name."
Then pray the Lord's Prayer

Introduction

Often organizers of concerts involving major celebrities will book lesser known acts to precede the featured celebrity. The lesser known acts warm up the crowd to prepare them for the main event.

1. How might a lesser known musician, comedian, or musical group prepare a crowd for the main event?

2. Although the warmup acts may be less famous, why is it important that their performances be of good quality?

In today's lesson we witness God's warmup activity through the work of John the Baptizer, who prepared the crowds for the person and work of the promised Messiah. John's warning to repent prepared people to receive, through faith, the forgiveness of sins and eternal life Jesus would earn for them through His death on the cross.

Study

Examine Luke 1:57–80 and Matthew 3:1–12.

Reading the Text

Thousands of years of history and hundreds of important and exciting Old Testament stories are the preparation for today's story. John is the forerunner, the warmup; Jesus is the fulfillment, the main event. God's care of Israel—delivering her from Egypt, settling her in the Promised Land, providing judges and kings, restoring her from captivity—all paved the way for the coming of Christ, the Savior. In this quarter's lessons Jesus arrives and establishes His gracious ministry. He is the Messiah God's people have been waiting for!

Elizabeth and her husband, the priest Zechariah, have their miracle baby (Luke 1:57–58). So remarkable is the boy's birth that friends throughout the hill country of Judea recognize it as a display of "great mercy" from the Lord. (Childlessness was often viewed as a curse among the ancient Jews.)

On the day the baby is circumcised, well-wishers are unable to accept Elizabeth's insistence that he be named John (1:59–62). The name is crucial; it had been commanded to Zechariah by the angel Gabriel (1:13). Its meaning, "the Lord is gracious," describes not only the gift that this child was to his longing parents, but also the greater gift that John will announce: the Christ. Zechariah cuts off all discussion (1:63–66). There's no room for debate. "His name is John." Notice how far Zechariah has come from the doubt he stammered to the angel nine months earlier (1:18). Now Zechariah understands. God has spoken. Case closed.

Filled by the Holy Spirit with this conviction (and at last able to speak after months of silence), Zechariah expresses his faith in words we still sing today (1:67–79). Known in the liturgies as the Benedictus (from the Latin word for "blessed"), Zechariah's prophecy is striking because it describes future events as if they had already happened. He speaks of Christ, a "horn of salvation" in the house of David (a horn represents strength as for a bull or a ram, 1 Samuel 2:10; Psalm 18:2, 89:17). The Savior promised long ago to Abraham, will deliver Israel from all her enemies, especially death (Luke 1:79). Jesus would not be born for several more months, and His atoning work would not be completed for another 33 years. Yet Zechariah proclaims that God "has come and has redeemed His people" (1:68). Such was John's mission that his coming assured Christ's saving work.

Zechariah's boy would be that final "prophet of the Most High" (1:76) who would "prepare the way" for the Messiah, Israel's "rising sun" of righteousness (1:78). Zechariah had in mind the closing prophesies of the Old Testament (Malachi 4:6). John would come as a new Elijah (Malachi 4:5; cf. Luke 1:17; Matthew 17:9–13) to usher in the One who would fulfill the law of Moses (Malachi 4:4). With John's birth, all this was now certain.

Nevertheless, for the next 30 years, John lived in obscurity (Luke 1:80). Very likely, his departure for the desert came after the death of his elderly parents, while he was still quite young. He may have spent these years among the Essenes, a strict Jewish sect from whom today we have the Dead Sea Scrolls. (A considerable time did indeed lapse between John's and Jesus' birth and their public appearances.)

When John did finally make his entrance, it was with a splash (Matthew 3:1–12). The best historical calculations set John's arrival in A.D. 26, a sabbatical year, in which Jews were released from business and agriculture (Leviticus 25:15). Thus freed from many everyday responsibilities, the crowds flocked to the Jordan. They found a prophet whose appearance reminded them of Elijah (Matthew 3:4; 2 Kings 1:8) and whose preaching had the same power.

John's message ("Repent, for the kingdom of heaven is near") is often characterized as fiery preaching of the Law. Certainly it was that (Matthew 3:7–12), and it was effective (Luke 3:10–14). But the real heart of John's message was in fact Gospel. To proclaim the kingdom of heaven near was to answer the deepest longing of the faithful. The coming of the kingdom meant nothing less than the arrival of the Messiah, the One who would establish God's rule for all eternity and enable believers to share in it as kings themselves. In other words, everything to which the Old Testament had pointed was now imminent.

The Gospel writers emphasize this in their descriptions of John. Previously connected with Elijah, and Malachi, he is now also the one referred to by Isaiah (Matthew 3:3; Isaiah 40:3). John is obviously the culmination of all of the Old Testament prophets. It could go no further. All that could remain was the Messiah Himself.

In preparation for the Christ, then, many people were baptized. Like Christian Baptism today, John's baptism gave forgiveness of all sins (Mark 1:4). In this way, it made the recipients ready for the One "more powerful" than John who would separate believers from unbelievers as a farmer separates wheat from chaff (Matthew 3:11–12). Believers in Him, those who had received this forgiveness, Christ would bless with His Holy Spirit; those who were not prepared with faith He would cast into unquenchable fire. And as the entire narrative of John attests, the time for preparation was now!

Discussing the Text

1. Compare the reaction in Luke 1:58 with the reaction you would expect today after the birth of a baby.

2. What is the significance of the name *John?*

3. Reread Luke 1:67–79. How does Zechariah's song of praise reveal his understanding of God's plan?

4. How was John's ministry a warmup for the main event?

5. What message of Law and Gospel did John proclaim in Matthew 3:7–11?

6. How did John's baptism prepare the people for the Messiah?

Apply

The story of John the Baptist, in keeping with the theme of Advent, always delivers a warning: Repent! As Christ was soon to come in John's day, so He will return very soon at the end of the world. That Last Day may in fact be generations away, but for every soul it is nevertheless immediate. The judgment is always as near as our own death, and no one can be certain that it will not be today. Therefore, we desire that our lives be marked by a constant resolve to turn away from sin in true repentance.

True repentance, though, cannot be motivated by fear of judgment alone. While the certainty of punishment can bring contrition and terror of conscience, true repentance has another component as well: faith. Along with contrition, repentance includes trust that God is forgiving for Jesus' sake. Here the words of John and his father, Zechariah, are even more important. Both remind us that Christ's forgiveness is always immediate. For Zechariah, God's redemption in the Messiah was an accomplished fact even before Jesus was born. To John, the kingdom of grace was "near," just as present. When God's people, moved by the warning of His Law, realize their sin, they can always be sure that their forgiveness in Christ is also an accomplished fact, even a present reality.

That, in turn, enables us to enjoy the other message of John and of Advent: the future fulfillment. For the forgiven sinner, Christ's second Advent holds no fear, but rather eager anticipation. We look forward to being gathered "into the barn" as the precious wheat of Christ's harvest (Matthew 3:12).

1. Read Romans 3:20 and 1:16. What is the purpose of God's Law? What is the purpose of God's Gospel?

2. How does our faith in Christ Jesus enable us to look forward to Jesus' return on Judgment Day with peace and joy?

3. The Lord's Supper is often called "a foretaste of the feast to come." How is the Lord's Supper a warmup for the main event?

4. Reflect on your Baptism. How did God prepare you for life on this earth? Life with Him forever through Baptism?

Catechism Connection

Examine David's prayer used in the opening for this session.

1. We find the Lord's Prayer in Matthew 6:9–13 and Luke 11:2–4. Some manuscripts include the following words at the end of Matthew 6:13: "for Yours is the kingdom and the power and the glory forever. Amen." Whether or not Jesus actually spoke these words, why is it appropriate to include them in the Lord's Prayer? See 1 Chronicles 29:10–13 and Mark 16:19.

2. What benefit of Jesus' rule do we find in Ephesians 2:10?

3. What benefit of Jesus' rule do we find in Philippians 4:6–7?

Send

To Do This Week

Family Connection

1. Remember each family member's Baptism. Discuss the power and the blessings God provided you at your Baptism.

2. Review the events of John the Baptist's life and ministry. Discuss how he prepared people to receive Jesus. Share how you might prepare people to receive the gift of faith in Christ Jesus.

3. Reread Zechariah's song of praise (Luke 1:67–79). Get out a pen or pencil and a sheet of paper and write a family song of praise. Call the finished song of praise "The [Name of Your Family) Song of Praise."

Personal Reflection

1. Remember your Baptism each morning as you awake and each night as you go to bed. Make the sign of the cross and say, "In the name of God the Father, God the Son, and God the Holy Spirit."

2. Meditate on the words of Zechariah's song.

3. Consider as you receive the Lord's Supper how the Lord is providing you a warmup for the main event.

For Next Week

Read Luke 1:26–55 in preparation for the next session.

Session 2

An Angel Visits Mary

(Luke 1:26–55)

Gather

Theme: Highly Favored

Key Point

God in His love for us chose to send His only Son to earth to accomplish that which we would be unable to accomplish on our own—forgiveness of sins and eternal life.

Objectives

By the power of the Holy Spirit working through God's Word we will

1. describe the events surrounding the Annunciation and Mary's response;
2. compare Mary's response to the message of the angel to Zechariah's response;
3. explain how we have received a highly favored status with God;
4. write a song of praise and thanksgiving in response to the grace God has demonstrated to us through Christ Jesus.

Opening

Speak together the Second Article of the Apostles' Creed:
[I believe] in Jesus Christ, His only Son, our Lord, who was conceived by the Holy Spirit, born of the Virgin Mary, suffered under Pontius Pilate, was crucified, died and was buried. He descended into hell. The third day He rose again from the dead. He ascended into heaven and sits at the right hand of God, the Father Almighty. From thence He will come to judge the living and the dead.

Introduction

Today countries around the world seek a highly favored trade status with other countries.

1. What are the benefits of a highly favored status?

2. What does a country have to do to receive a highly favored status?

3. How would you describe your status before God? Why?

In today's lesson we witness how God chose Mary, an ordinary, sinful person to receive a highly favored status with Him. Through Christ, God continues to provide most favored status to all who believe in Jesus—His person and His work.

Study

Examine Luke 1:26–55.

Reading the Text

For the extraordinary event on which all eternity would turn—and from which the world would come to mark its time—God chose an ordinary young woman. With a beauty perhaps unmatched in Scripture, the story of the angel's visit to Mary begins the greatest story ever told; it demonstrates just how gracious God really is.

Six months after announcing to Zechariah that he and Elizabeth would have a son, the angel Gabriel was sent on another mission from God, this time to Nazareth in the region of Galilee (Luke

1:26). Because it was in Galilee, the northern province of Palestine, well-removed from Jerusalem, Nazareth was a most unlikely place for any significant development in Jewish religious history (John 1:46; 7:41, 52; also 1 Kings 9:11–13; Isaiah 9:1–2).

Even less likely was the choice of the woman to whom Gabriel was sent (Luke 1:27). Mary was a poor girl, as evidenced by the offering she and Joseph brought after Jesus' birth (compare Luke 2:22–24 with Leviticus 12:6–8). Recently engaged (see the discussion of Jewish engagement and marriage in Lesson 3), she was likely in her early teens. Mary was not unusually wise, gifted, or steeped in good works; certainly she was not without sin. In fact, knowing her own unworthiness, she was taken aback when the angel called her "highly favored" (Luke 1:28–29). Mary was only one of the pious Jewish maidens of her generation and those past.

She was, though, of the royal line of David, as was her fiancé. Obviously that was not something she had achieved herself either, but it did identify her as eligible for the most unique honor Gabriel was to announce. Every Jew knew that the Messiah would come from the family of David (2 Samuel 7:8–17). For a thousand years, that precious line had survived idolatry (1 Kings 11:4–8; 29–33), rebellion (1 Kings 12:16–19), assassinations (2 Kings 12:19–21; 14:18–21), deportation (2 Kings 24:10–15; 25:27–30), and dispersion (Jeremiah 23:1–5; Ezra 1:1–4). Clearly God's hand had been at work. But by the time of Mary and Joseph, the Davidic line held no throne; it had no present glory to show for its past greatness.

All this would suddenly change through the birth of David's heir. Mary, the angel declares, would bear a son and name Him Jesus (Luke 1:30–31). The name alone suggests great things. Jesus (Yeshua in Hebrew) is the Greek form of the same name given by Moses to his successor, known to us as Joshua (Numbers 13:16). Meaning "the Lord is salvation," it marked Mary's son as the Savior. (Joshua, too, had been a kind of savior, leading Israel in its conquest of the Promised Land.)

But this Yeshua would be much more. "He will be great," Gabriel said (Luke 1:32), echoing the words Micah had used to describe One whose "goings forth are from the days of eternity" (Micah 5:2—see NIV note). Most significant, He would be "the Son of the Most High" and the son of "His father David." Mary's son would be like none other in all eternity: true God and true man. He would not only restore the glory of David's dynasty; He would establish its majesty forever (Luke 1:33).

Mary's reaction is priceless (1:34). The angel has been speaking of God's cosmic purpose. Mary's concern is the natural order: "How is this all going to happen? I'm a virgin." The infinite, eternal implications are beyond her. Yet she will gladly entrust them to God. She puzzles only the immediate effect on herself and her future.

Gently, then, the messenger explains (1:35–37). Yes, Mary would still be a virgin, but the Holy Spirit would accomplish the miracle. In this way, the baby would be truly Mary's son and God's Son. As further assurance (which Mary had not requested), the angel offered the example of Elizabeth, a cousin or aunt of Mary's, who seemingly also could not be having a baby. "With God nothing will be impossible" (NKJV).

In humble faith Mary accepts God's will (1:38). It is not an easy assignment! Who would believe her explanation when the pregnancy became evident? Elizabeth would understand (1:39–45). So would Elizabeth's unborn child, for, as Gabriel had told Zechariah, John had been filled with the Holy Spirit while still in his mother's womb (1:15). (John's faith prior to birth may be an exceptional case, but it surely is another reminder that the unborn are always living souls.)

Mary's song (1:46–55), called the Magnificat, poetically summarizes the theme of the entire story. Mary exalts the Lord because He has regarded someone as lowly as she. The proud He has sent empty away, but the humble He has lifted up and filled with good things. Mary grasps the reason God has chosen her to be the mother of the Lord: it is by His grace alone.

Discussing the Text

1. What characteristics of God do you find in the fact that He chose such an unlikely woman (Mary) from such an unlikely place (Nazareth) to be the mother of the Lord?

2. What characteristics of Mary do you find in her responses in Luke 1:29, 34, and 38?

3. How was God's hand evident in selecting Mary, considering the promise He made to David many years before?

4. What is the significance of the name Gabriel tells Mary to call her son?

5. Compare Mary's reaction to Gabriel's message to Zechariah's reaction (Luke 1:18).

6. Describe in your own words the content of Mary's song of praise.

Apply

Today's lesson makes vivid the all-important truth of grace—God's love for undeserving souls. Mary had in no way merited selection as the mother of the Savior, but God chose her anyway.

That is grace. We may feel insecure socially; we may feel inadequate for the demands of daily life; we may not see how we can play meaningful roles in God's kingdom. Yet as God chose Mary for His purpose, He also has chosen us. As God equipped a teenager for a once-in-all-history task, He is giving us whatever it takes to do what He plans for us. Yes, we are unworthy, inadequate in ourselves because we are sinners, like Mary. But in His grace God looks on us as His servants in our special callings.

Much more important, though, God's grace is evident in the fact that He gave His Son to become a baby. All humankind was undeserving of God's visitation. Because of sin, all of us deserve only to be cut off from God's attention forever. Instead, "He has been mindful of the humble state of His servant" (Luke 1:48). By sending His Son to be born into the world, God showed that He loves His creatures in spite of their sinfulness and that He will do everything necessary to save them. Jesus' coming to earth points directly to the cross—where grace is revealed to the full extent. God loves us so much that He gave His only begotten Son (KJV) for our forgiveness and everlasting life.

1. Although we may feel insecure, inadequate, or unimportant what assurance does God provide us in today's lesson?

2. All who believe in Christ have received a highly favored status before God. Summarize in your own words what this fact means for your life.

3. What does God sending His Son to die for you reveal about His love for you and all people?

4. God had prophesied the virgin birth of His Son. How does His fulfillment of that prophecy affect you?

Catechism Connection

Examine the Second Article of the Creed from the opening for this session.

1. Jesus was "conceived by the Holy Spirit." What additional information about His conception do you find in Matthew 1:25? Why is this information important?

2. Through the conception that was taking place in Mary's body, true God was becoming true man. What human characteristics does Scripture reveal in the following references: Matthew 4:2? 26:38? 27:50? Mark 4:38? Luke 24:39? John 11:35? 19:28?

Send

To Do This Week

Family Connection

1. Review the miraculous and marvelous events revealed in Luke 1:26–55.

2. Discuss how God sent Jesus for all people. Sit in a circle and say a brief prayer. Thank God for sending Jesus to die on the cross for the person sitting on your right: "Thank You, God, for sending Your Son, Jesus, to die on the cross for [name of the person sitting on your right]."

3. Ask, "Since we are highly favored by God through faith in Jesus, how can we demonstrate to others that we regard them as highly favored?" Identify one action each family member can do alone or with the family this week.

Personal Reflection

1. Reread Mary's song of praise. Reflect on the goodness God has provided to you through Jesus.

2. Write on a note card "I am highly favored by God through Christ." Place the note card in a conspicuous place, where you will see it often.

3. Share with someone who doesn't know Jesus the highly favored status you have received through Jesus. How does this status effect you as you live each day of your life? As you anticipate your physical death someday?

For Next Week

Read Matthew 1:18–25 and Isaiah 7:10–14 in preparation for the next session.

Session 3

Jesus Is Born

(Matthew 1:18–25; Isaiah 7:10–14)

Gather

Theme: God Intervenes!

Key Point

God in His love for us developed a perfect plan—a plan that defied all human understanding—to intervene in the lives of people with the life, death, and resurrection of His only Son, who alone could accomplish salvation for all.

Objectives

By the power of the Holy Spirit working through God's Word we will

1. describe the miraculous events leading up to and including the birth of Jesus;
2. identify how God intervened in the lives of Mary and Joseph to fulfill His plan for saving the world from sin;
3. explain how God continues to intervene in the lives of people today;
4. tell others of God's intervention in our lives.

Opening

Read Martin Luther's explanation to the Second Article of the Apostles' Creed responsively:

All: I believe that Jesus Christ, true God, begotten of the Father from eternity, and also true man, born of the virgin Mary, is my Lord,

Group 2: who has redeemed me, a lost and condemned person, purchased and won me from all sins, from death, and from the power of the devil; not with gold or silver, but with His holy, precious blood and with His innocent suffering and death,

Introduction

Intervention! Often people will intervene in the lives of others to help and to encourage them when they face difficult times, temptations, and hardships.

1. Describe how you or someone you know has intervened in someone's life. What was the result?

2. How has someone intervened in your life when you have faced difficulties? What was the result?

3. What motivates people to intervene in the lives of others?

In today's lesson we witness God intervening in the lives of Mary and Joseph to fulfill His promised plan of salvation. By His plan Jesus intervenes in the lives of all people, providing the means through which they can receive and enjoy the forgiveness of sins and eternal life.

Study

Examine Matthew 1:18–25 and Isaiah 7:10–14.

Reading the Text

Mary would have a son and yet remain a virgin. It was easy enough to say, and in His almighty power God would certainly be able to do it. But believing in the virgin birth would not be easy—either for the man most immediately involved or for future generations in a scientific age. And though it is expressed in simple words, Jesus' being "born of the virgin Mary" is an essential doctrine of our Christian faith. For in this way God chose to send His son, the Savior from sin, God with us!

After three months with Elizabeth (Luke 1:56), Mary faced the painful reality of returning home. Her pregnancy would soon be visible to all, and she could not expect family, friends, or neighbors to believe her explanation. Above all, she would have to explain to Joseph, her fiancé. Would he accept her story?

Scripture gives us no details of the dialog between Mary and Joseph. Surely she repeated to him the words of the angel, and surely he wanted to believe her.

If the worst be assumed, Mary had not just been guilty of violating the trust of engagement. She was guilty of a capital offense—adultery by a married woman. Engagement among the Jews carried the very same obligations as marriage itself. An engaged couple were husband and wife, although they did not yet cohabit. Vows had already been exchanged, a dowry presented, and the contract formalized in writing or orally, with a coin given as pledge. The betrothal would have been sealed with a benediction over a ceremonial cup of wine—all very solemn. For perhaps a number of months following, the groom would build a house, establish his business, or otherwise prepare to take his bride. In the meantime, of course, both were to remain chaste; according to Mosaic law, an engaged woman guilty of adultery would be stoned (Deuteronomy 22:20–21, 23–24).

In truth, by Joseph's day the death penalty was seldom imposed. Yet neither was an engagement easily terminated. The couple would go through a regular divorce. This is the course of action Joseph had determined (Matthew 1:18–19). He loved Mary. A quiet divorce, settled without charges or reasons given (Deuteronomy 24:1), would avoid disgracing Mary, would spare her life, and would let him get on with his.

But God intervenes (Matthew 1:20–21). An angelic messenger comes in a dream, as Joseph sleeps. (Dreams were a commonly accepted—even expected—means of divine communication among the Jews; see Genesis 28:12; 37:5–11; 40:8; 41:15; Numbers 12:6; 1 Samuel 28:6; Daniel 2:26; 4:18; 7:1). This time the angel's name is not given, but it may well have been Gabriel once more.

Immediately he seized Joseph's attention by calling him "son of David," a title specifically applied to the Messiah. Joseph was of David's lineage, but this greeting meant more. Joseph was to have a unique role in God's fulfilling the messianic promise. How? Through the baby conceived in Mary's womb. Mary's story was true: the conception was a miracle worked by the Holy Spirit.

Joseph could have believed his beloved all along, because this is precisely how God had promised long ago that His Son would be born (Matthew 1:22–23). Through Isaiah the prophet seven centuries earlier, God had offered wicked King Ahaz a sign that the Lord would deliver Judah from invaders. Ahaz had rejected the offer, choosing to seek help in an alliance with Assyria rather than in the Lord. So God instead gave a sign that would be fulfilled in the distant future: "The virgin will be with child and will give birth to a son, and will call His name Immanuel" (Isaiah 7:10–14).

The virgin birth of Christ defies scientific verification since it is a one-time, unrepeatable event. But it is both true and essential. Wonderfully, as the virgin-born son of Mary, Jesus is indeed Immanuel, God with us (Matthew 1:23). And that is a double-rich assurance. On the one hand, "Immanuel" reminds us that God is present with His people: He lived among them, as one of them, understands them, cares for them, fulfilled the Law for them, and died in their place. On the other hand, "Immanuel" teaches that it is nothing less than God who is with us. (*El* is Hebrew for "God.") The One who is with us is also powerful enough—as almighty God—to do great things for those He has visited.

Above all, He is powerful to save from sin, for this is the respect in which this Yeshua (Jesus) is the Savior (1:21). Saving from sin is, ultimately, the whole mission of Christ.

Dutifully, Joseph did his part (1:24–25). Very soon he would begin to see just what an adventure he was to share (Luke 2:1–20).

Discussing the Text

1. Why is the virgin birth of Jesus an essential doctrine of the Christian faith?

2. Evaluate the actions and attitudes of Joseph before he received the message from the angel (Matthew 1:18–19).

3. Evaluate Joseph's actions and attitudes after he received the message (1:24–25).

4. What assurance does the name *Immanuel* provide us?

5. Discuss the importance of the prophecy of Isaiah 7:10–14 being fulfilled in the events described in Matthew 1:18–25.

Apply

Today's Bible story offers at least three lessons that may be outstanding for us to learn. First, this is the text that most clearly exposes the all-important doctrine of the virgin birth. In an age in which this teaching is so often ridiculed, we must see and understand its biblical basis. The virgin birth is one of the fundamental facts every Christian needs to know.

Second, Jesus' name is a useful handle to remember His forgiveness. That Jesus saves us from our sin is more than something to be known. It is the core doctrine of the Christian faith that must be trusted. What better way to hold Jesus' salvation uppermost in mind than to learn that His very name means Savior!

Finally, the twin emphases of Immanuel, God with us, can be of daily comfort to us. God is here present in our lives every minute, and that He understands our every need because He once lived with us on earth. The One who knows and understands us so well is God Himself, the One who can always do something about our needs.

1. How can Jesus' name be useful for us daily?

2. To believe that which is impossible to believe—that is what God enabled Joseph to do. How does God continue to work today to enable people to believe that which may seem impossible to believe?

3. What are some blessings you or others have received because God intervened in your life or the lives of others?

4. How might or how has God used you as His agent of intervention?

Catechism Connection

Examine Martin Luther's explanation of the Second Article from the opening for this session.

1. Mary gave birth to a real human baby—true man. Why was it necessary for Jesus to be true man? See Galatians 4:4–5; Hebrews 2:14. It was necessary that this infant also be true God. Why? See Psalm 49:7; Mark 10:45; and 1 Corinthians 15:57.

2. What divine attributes of Jesus are revealed in the following passages? Matthew 28:18; 28:20; John 1:1–2; 21:17; Hebrews 13:8.

3. Which of these attributes do you especially appreciate today?

Send

To Do This Week

Family Connection

1. Review the miraculous events of Matthew 1:18–25 with your family. Ask, "How was God active in the lives of Mary and Joseph?" Then ask, "How is God active in our lives today?"

2. Write *Immanuel* on a large sheet of paper. Underneath the word write, *God with us.* Then let members of the family write what this means to them on the sheet of paper.

3. Pray together, thanking God for sending a Savior.

Personal Reflection

1. Meditate on the name Jesus. Give thanks to God for sending a Savior.

2. Share the meaning of the name *Jesus* with a friend or loved one.

3. Write *Immanuel* on a note card. Place the note card in your wallet. When you face trials, troubles, or temptations pull out the card and remember that the name means "God with us."

For Next Week

Read Matthew 2:1–12 in preparation for the next session.

Session 4

Wise Men Worship Jesus

(Matthew 2:1–12)

Gather

Theme: Inclusive: for Everyone

Key Point

Jesus' love is inclusive. His death on the cross won salvation for everyone.

Objectives

By the power of the Holy Spirit working through God's Word we will

1. describe the events of the visit of the Magi, the Wise Men;
2. explain how the visit of the Magi reveals God's inclusive plan for salvation;
3. explain why the star of this account is God and the Magi are simply filling supporting roles;
4. seek new ways to share Jesus' love with all people.

Opening

Speak together the words of Isaiah 42:6–7.
"I, the LORD, have called you in righteousness;
I will take hold of your hand.
I will keep you and will make you
to be a covenant for the people
and a light for the Gentiles,
to open eyes that are blind,
to free captives from prison
and to release from the dungeon those who sit in
darkness."

Introduction

1. What words come to mind when you hear the word *inclusive?* Write them.

2. What words that you have written seem to go together? Group them.

3. Write a one-word label for each group of words.

4. Now write a one- or two-sentence definition of *inclusive* using the labels.

Inclusive describes the message of today's lesson. Jesus came to earth to win salvation for all people.

Study

Examine Matthew 2:1–12.

Reading the Text

The story of the Wise Men is one of the best known in all of Scripture. Most people recognize the three figures of the Christmas crèche, bearing gifts, kneeling before Christ. It's appropriate that everyone should know the story, because the message of the Magi's visit is that everyone is welcomed in Christ's kingdom. *Epiphany,* as this event is called (from the Greek word for "appearing or revealing"), proclaims that Jesus is the Savior of the Jews *and* the Gentiles.

Surprisingly, we know very little about the Wise Men; we do not know who they were or where they came from. We do not know their names or even their number. The truth is, the Bible reveals precious few details about the Wise Men, and that was surely the Holy Spirit's intent, because the Wise Men are not the stars of the story.

Matthew's account begins with the arrival of travelers in Jerusalem (2:1–2). No names are given, no head count taken. (The names Gaspar, Melchior, and Balthasar are late tradition and quite unlikely, and the text never specifies that there were three men).

All Matthew discloses is that the visitors were "magi," members of a caste of wise men who studied the heavenly bodies as well as medicine and other natural sciences. While some magi were the legitimate scholars of the day, all practiced astrology, often to advise kings. (In Daniel 2:1–3 they are called "astrologers" or "Chaldeans." They themselves were almost surely not kings, although this has been mistakenly inferred from Isaiah 60:1–6, Psalm 72:10–11 and other passages.) Such men were prominent in Babylonia, Persia, Media, and Arabia, any of which could have been the home of these particular "Wise Men from the east."

What had led them to seek the King of the Jews? They had seen "His star" and came to worship Him. The Greek word for *star* actually includes virtually any major light in the night sky. This "star" may, therefore, have been a rare conjunction of Jupiter and Saturn—and later also Mars—which occurred in 7 B.C. and is repeated only about every 800 years. However, the "star" of Bethlehem appears to have moved in such a way as to have been a unique miracle (Matthew 2:9). In either case, God was commanding the heavens to declare Christ's birth.

Having seen the star, the Wise Men somehow deduced that it was the sign of a new king in Judea. That conclusion was probably based on a reading of Numbers 24:17: "A star will come out of Jacob; a scepter will rise out of Israel." (The captivity and dispersion of the Jews made the Old Testament writings available to serious scholars in the major eastern courts of the ancient world.)

Still remarkable, though, is the fact that these Gentiles came seeking a Jewish king. This was not a mere courtesy call, a diplomatic mission dispatched by a fellow crowned head. "King of the Jews" was one of the numerous technical titles for the Messiah, the Savior and King of Israel (Jeremiah 23:5–6; Zechariah 9:9). The Magi came not to visit just any king. They came to worship the King promised by God in His Word.

Unfortunately, the reason for the Magi's visit did not sit well with the earthly king of the Jewish nation (Matthew 2:3). Herod the Great is known to history as a shrewd politician who nimbly shifted his allegiance among, variously, Julius Caesar, Mark Antony, Cleopatra, Augustus, and the Jewish religious establishment. He was an energetic builder, and spent lavishly on public projects (the new Jerusalem temple was an architectural marvel). Herod was also known as a cruel and jealous madman who murdered his favorite wife, several of his children, and then was haunted by dreams of their death. Herod was actually Idumean, not Jewish. Yet by Roman decree he ruled with the title *king of the Jews* for some 33 years.

Naturally Herod was suspicious of anyone with a more legitimate claim to the throne. Without revealing his motives, he asked the priests and teachers where, according to the Scriptures, the Messiah was to be born (2:5–6). Micah 5:2 provided the clear answer, but they cited it with a significant update. Bethlehem was, according to Micah's prophecy, "small among the clans of Judah." That was, of course, true in an earthly, numerical sense. In reality, though, the priests and scribes said Bethlehem was "by no means least among the rulers of Judah" (Matthew 2:6), for the birth of the Christ would forever make it great in God's plans.

Satisfied that he knew the whereabouts of his target, Herod now investigated when the child was born (2:7). From his wicked order not many days later (2:16), it seems the Wise Men must have reported first seeing the star some time earlier (2:8). Thus, when the Wise Men arrived in Bethlehem (2:9–11), they did not come to a stable to find adoring shepherds and a baby in a manger. They found the holy family in a house, possibly going about ordinary life, with Joseph taking up work as a carpenter in Bethlehem.

The joy they felt (2:10) was that of spiritual travelers who had reached eternal peace. Before a little child, in a simple house that denied any earthly power or glory, they prostrated themselves. They knew that Jesus' kingdom was not of this world (John 18:36). They worshiped Him as the heavenly Savior—their Savior.

The three gifts (from which arose the tradition of three Wise Men) expressed their faith and joy of salvation. Intended or not, the gifts may also have symbolized the person and work of Jesus: gold befitting a king; frankincense, since it was burned in worship, reminding that Jesus is true God; and myrrh, a sweet- smelling gum used to prepare bodies for burial (John 19:39–40), an apt symbol of His redeeming death.

Perhaps the Wise Men grasped none of that significance. Nevertheless, as they left for home having been warned by God to avoid Herod (Matthew 2:12), they no doubt returned as the shepherds had earlier (Luke 2:20), praising God and satisfied that they, too, were accepted as subjects of the Great King.

Discussing the Text

1. Read Numbers 24:17 and Jeremiah 23:5–6. If these words led the Wise Men to seek "the king of the Jews" (Matthew 2:2), what does this reveal about Balaam and Jeremiah? about Jewish people who lived in other parts of the world? about God?

2. Who were the Magi? How is their identity somewhat different than that revealed in the familiar Christmas carol "We Three Kings of Orient Are"?

3. Why was Herod concerned about that which the Wise Men revealed to him concerning the new king?

4. What were the three gifts given by the Wise Men? What might these have symbolized? How would this symbolism show God's action?

5. How was God active in the lives of the Wise Men (Matthew 2:12)?

6. What does the account of the Wise Men reveal about God's attitude toward inclusivity?

7. How does this entire account reveal the truth of 1 Timothy 2:4?

Apply

The coming of the Wise Men is indeed the revelation that Gentiles as well as Jews belong to Christ's kingdom. But it is no accident that Matthew reveals so little about the Wise Men themselves. For it is not, properly speaking, the Wise Men's coming that demonstrates the inclusiveness of the Kingdom. It is God's inviting that shows we are all included. More than the Wise Men, the star and the Child it pointed to are the center of the story. God placed the star in the sky to call people from distant lands to the Savior. God's placing the star in the sky assures us that we do not come to Christ's birthday without an invitation, but as guests of honor.

If the Wise Men, Gentiles for whom no other qualifications are given, are welcome before Christ, then everyone is welcome, too. Whether she feels like, looks like, speaks like others, whether he is a model citizen or a gang member, she or he is invited to be Christ's own through faith. Epiphany reveals that Jesus came for everyone!

1. What is the significance of that which God reveals in the account of the Wise Men for you? For all people? See Galatians 3:26–28.

2. How are we "guests of honor" at the celebration of Jesus' birth?

3. How does the welcome that God offers to us—the chief of sinners for whom Jesus died—affect our witness of faith to others?

4. What is our congregation doing to welcome all types of people? What else might we do?

Catechism Connection

Examine Martin Luther's explanation of the Second Article from the opening for Session 3.

1. God anointed Jesus (Acts 10:38) to be our Prophet, Priest, and King. Read John 6:68. What does Jesus do as Prophet?

2. What do Hebrews 7:26–27 and 1 John 2:1 reveal about Jesus' actions as Priest?

3. Describe Jesus' kingship as He revealed it through His message to Pilate (John 18:36–37).

Send

To Do This Week

Family Connection

1. Reread Matthew 2:1–12. Discuss how God was active in the account. How was God the star in the account?

2. Jesus came for all people. How does this fact reassure us? What does this fact say to us concerning telling others of Jesus' love?

3. Write "For All People" on a large sheet of newsprint. Then as a family draw pictures of those for whom Jesus came to earth. Or cut out pictures of all kinds of people from magazines and glue them to the sheet of paper.

4. Talk about how you might better share Jesus' love with all people.

5. Cut a star from a piece of poster board. Decorate the star. Tape it on your shirt. When people ask you the reason you are wearing the star, tell them that God has made you a star through His Son's death on the cross.

Personal Reflection

1. Meditate on the concept of inclusiveness. Pray, thanking God that He has included you—a poor miserable sinner—in His plan for salvation.

2. Identify ways in which God continues to be a star today.

For Next Week

Read Matthew 2:13–23 in preparation for the next session.

Session 5

Mary and Joseph Take Jesus to Egypt

(Matthew 2:13–23)

Gather

Theme: God's Itinerary

Key Point

The Holy Spirit, working through the means of grace—God's Word and Sacraments—strengthens our faith so that nothing can separate us from the love of God in the person and work of Jesus.

Objectives

By the power of the Holy Spirit working through God's Word we will

1. describe how God enables His itinerary—plan of salvation—to be accomplished in spite of Herod's attempts to undermine it;
2. explain how God continues to enable His itinerary—His plan of salvation—to be accomplished in the lives of His people today in spite of Satan's, the world's, and our own sinful attempts to undermine it;
3. seek opportunities to strengthen our faith through the means of grace to enable *God's* itinerary for our lives to be *our* itineraries.

Opening

Read the First Article of the Apostles' Creed and Martin Luther's explanation responsively:

All: I believe in God, the Father Almighty, Maker of heaven and earth.

Leader: What does this mean?

Group 1: I believe that God has made me and all creatures; that He has given me my body and soul, eyes, ears, and all my members, my reason and all my senses, and still takes care of them.

Group 2: He also gives me clothing and shoes, food and drink, house and home, wife and children, land, animals, and all I have. He richly and daily provides me with all that I need to support this body and life.

Group 1: He defends me against all danger and guards and protects me from all evil.

Group 2: All this He does only out of fatherly, divine goodness and mercy, without any merit or worthiness in me. For all this it is my duty to thank and praise, serve and obey Him.

All: This is most certainly true.

Introduction

1. What is God's itinerary for your life?

2. What factors sometimes work to challenge His itinerary for your life?

3. Nothing "will be able to separate us from the love of God that is in Christ Jesus our Lord" (Romans 8:39). What promise does St. Paul give to you from God in this passage concerning God's itinerary for your life? How do these words give you comfort as you face temptations from Satan, the world, and your sinful self?

In today's lesson, evil Herod attempts to destroy God's itinerary. But God's itinerary—plan for salvation—cannot and will not be stopped. Jesus will not die as an infant at the hands of Herod. Instead, God's itinerary for Jesus to die a more ferocious death on the cross will be accomplished, and in this act God will win forgiveness of sins and eternal life for all.

Study

Examine Matthew 2:13–23.

Reading the Text

God's plan for our salvation was now in motion, and nothing would derail it. Devilish opposition, in the person of King Herod, would go to any lengths to prevent the newborn King from claiming His rightful throne. But today's lesson demonstrates that at every turn God remains in control, guiding every move, directing each step, toward His intended result.

God's direction is made clear by the prominence, once more, of dreams (Matthew 2:13, 19, 22). Nothing happens by chance, nor can human scheming thwart God's designs. In the dream that begins today's story, in fact, God anticipates and preempts Herod's plot: "Herod is going to search for the child to kill Him" (2:13).

God's command was urgent: "Get up!" Joseph's immediate obedience—"during the night"—essential. Herod would not wait many days for the Wise Men to return; surely this matter of a rival king fully occupied his deranged mind. And Bethlehem was only about five miles from Jerusalem. Herod's soldiers could arrive within an hour!

Seemingly driven by Herod's threat, the flight to Egypt was actually God's itinerary. God fully intended to bring His Son out of Egypt (2:15). Matthew proves this by quoting the Old Testament (Hosea 11:1), as he so often does (at least 47 times). Certainly Hosea's prophecy referred to Israel's exodus from slavery, but Israel itself was always to be a prophecy of Christ. Jesus, Matthew understands, is the fulfillment of the entire Old Testament history.

Herod was enraged! Scholars have estimated that perhaps 20 baby boys, two and under, would have lived in Bethlehem and its environs. His order to kill the children earned Herod notoriety in the ancient world: among the early Christians, abortion was known as "Herodism." (The Holy Innocents are still remembered in a festival of the church on December 28.)

Herod's wickedness knew no bounds, but it would avail him nothing against God's course. Herod was nearing his own end. In 4 B.C., likely within months of the Bethlehem murders, he would be stricken with an emaciating disease. Fearing that no one would mourn his death, he gave one last crazed order: Thousands of Jewish nobles were called to the great hippodrome in Jericho. When all were assembled, the gates were blocked and the guards commanded to kill everyone inside as soon as Herod himself died. In this way, Herod reasoned, his death would be marked by weeping throughout the whole nation. Fortunately, once Herod was dead, the order was abandoned.

There was weeping enough for the babies of Bethlehem (2:17–18). This time Matthew's quotation (Jeremiah 31:15) describes the lamentation of Israel and Judah as they were carried into captivity centuries before. Rachel had been one of the mothers from whom the whole nation had grown (Genesis 46:8–27), and she had died en route to Bethlehem (Genesis 35:16–19). Ramah was a town at which captives were mustered for the long march to Babylon (Jeremiah 40:1). Thus the words of Jeremiah (and, again, the Old Testament events) typified a fulfillment in Christ's coming—the sorrows of Bethlehem's mothers for their children.

Meanwhile, Joseph very likely settled his family among one of the numerous Jewish communities in Egypt. The huge port city of Alexandria, for example, had more Jewish residents than Jerusalem. Jews made up some 40 percent of its population, and it had a large synagogue.

How long Jesus and His parents remained in Egypt is unknown. Like the command to flee, the command to relocate came from God in a dream (Matthew 2:19–21). Joseph and Mary likely planned to return to Bethlehem, but once more God intervened (2:22–23). Mary and Joseph feared Archelaus not simply because he was Herod's son. (Another of Herod's sons was ruling in Galilee, where they did indeed locate.) Archelaus had already proved himself a bloody tyrant in his own right, massacring 3,000 Jews in one incident shortly after taking power.

God provided the answer: the region of Galilee, Mary and Joseph's previous home of Nazareth. As always, God's hand is evident. It is difficult to be sure what "prophets" Matthew is citing in verse 23. He may be speaking of Old Testament prophets in general, who collectively described many aspects of the Messiah's origin. Or the reference may be to Isaiah 11:1, since the Hebrew root of Nazareth appears there as "Branch," a name for the Christ. Prophecy does, however, fix the region of the Messiah's appearing as Galilee (Isaiah 9:1–2; cf. Matthew 4:12–16). Thus even Archelaus' cruelty God used for His purpose. His Son was not to grow up in the more prominent Judea, but rather in the north country—in Nazareth.

Discussing the Text

1. How is God's control evident in the events of this lesson?

2. How does Hosea 11:1 indicate that the flight to Egypt was actually God's itinerary?

3. How were the words of Jeremiah 31:15 and Jeremiah 40:1 fulfilled in today's text?

4. How do the events in this account illustrate the truth of Romans 8:35–39?

Apply

Every development in the life of Christ leads to the climax of all God's designs. The Bethlehem babies are remembered as a picture of an infinitely more terrible tragedy. The infant Jesus was saved from death only so that He could die another day, in a far more horrible way. It was not God's plan to allow death at this time. God's Son would live so that He could take all our sins and all suffering to the cross.

Herod and his wicked descendants are long gone, but opposition to Christ and His purposes continue. That, of course, is because the real enemy is Satan. Every minute Jesus was on earth, the devil schemed to undermine His mission, and he plots with the same intensity against us. Bloodshed we hear, read about, and perhaps see; suffering we experience; sadness touches our families—all are deeds of Satan to frighten or discourage us.

Try as he does, though, Satan cannot prevent God's good will for us. Despite Herod's cunning and force, Jesus would grow up—in Egypt and then Galilee, as God had planned—in order to die the death of the cross, which God had also planned. All of that being accomplished and being followed by Jesus' resurrection, Satan has been defeated. God will have His way in our lives—above all in giving us the forgiveness and eternal life which Christ's death, according to the plan and will of God, has earned.

1. How are opposition to Jesus and His purpose still evident today?

2. What assurance does Jesus' death on the cross and glorious resurrection provide us as we face troubles, hardships, and temptations?

3. How do you witness God's itinerary for you by your words and actions?

4. How might you more effectively share with others God's itinerary for you and them?

5. When are some times when even Christians may question God's itinerary for them? How can you help people at such times?

Catechism Connection

Examine Martin Luther's explanation of the First Article from the opening for this session.

1. Read Genesis 37:28 and 50:20. Also skim the intervening chapters. What does this event demonstrate about God's care?

2. We may worry about things that could happen to us. In Matthew 6:25–34 Jesus discusses the futility of worry. What antidote does He recommend in verse 33?

Send

To Do This Week

Family Connection

1. Review the events of Matthew 2:13–23. Discuss how God was in control.

2. Prepare a chart with four columns: *My Problem, Solution Relying on My Control, Solution Relying on God's Control, Plan of Action*. Fill in all four columns for two or three problems. Check your progress on the action plan at the end of each day this week.

3. Discuss *itinerary*. What does someone's itinerary tell you about the important things in his/her life? How can we demonstrate through our family's itinerary that God is important in our lives?

Personal Reflection

1. Meditate on Romans 8:39. What comfort does this passage provide you as you face troubles, hardships, and temptations?

2. Give thanks to God for making you a number 1 priority in His itinerary.

3. Consider your weekly itinerary. How might you better reflect God's itinerary in your itinerary?

For Next Week

Read Matthew 3:13–17 in preparation for the next session.

Session 6

John Baptizes Jesus

(Matthew 3:13–17)

Gather

Theme: A Representative

Key Point

Jesus, as our representative before God, presents us sinless to God. We are assured through our Baptism that God accepts us as His own dear children, and that He will one day call us from this life to life eternal with Him in heaven.

Objectives

By the power of the Holy Spirit working through God's Word we will
1. describe the events leading up to and during Jesus' baptism;
2. explain how Jesus is our representative before God—a perfect representative who fulfilled all righteousness on our behalf;
3. confess the assurance that God provided to us in our Baptism.

Opening

Read together Martin Luther's explanation of the blessings of Baptism:

Leader: What benefits does Baptism give?

Group: It works forgiveness of sins, rescues from death and the devil, and gives eternal salvation to all who believe this, as the words and promises of God declare.

Leader: Which are these words and promises of God?

Group: Christ our Lord says in the last chapter of Mark: "Whoever believes and is baptized will be saved, but whoever does not believe will be condemned." [Mark 16:16]

Introduction

- Every three years, congregations of The Lutheran Church—Missouri Synod send representatives to District conventions.
- Every three years, every Circuit of The Lutheran Church—Missouri Synod sends representatives to a synodical convention.
- The United States and Canada each send a representative to the United Nations.
- Local voters biennially elect a representative to Congress.
1. Describe the job of a representative.

2. What must a representative do in order to be considered effective by the people she/he represents?

Jesus became our representative to fulfill all righteousness. In today's lesson we will discover how Jesus was and remains our perfect representative.

Study

Examine Matthew 3:13–17.

Reading the Text

With one exception (Luke 2:41–52), the Bible is silent about the years following Jesus' return from Egypt. When Jesus was about 30 years old, John the Baptizer arrived on the scene, preaching and baptizing in the Jordan River. After several months of ministry, John came to the northernmost point of his mission field, Bethany (or Bethabara, John 1:28; not the home of Mary, Martha, and Lazarus; John 11:1, 18). This site was only about 20 miles from Nazareth, and it was likely here that Jesus came to be baptized by John (Matthew 3:13).

Why would Jesus wish to be baptized? Initially John himself did not understand (3:14), for John's baptism was for the forgiveness of sins, and Jesus had no sin to be washed away. Jesus' explanation, that His baptism was "to fulfill all righteousness" (3:15), suggests at least three reasons.

First, Jesus' baptism, accompanied as it was by the voice and appearance of God the Father and God the Holy Spirit (3:16–17), was a public seal of approval of Jesus as the Messiah. *Messiah* (from the Hebrew, like *Christ* in Greek) means "Anointed One." At His baptism, Jesus was, in a unique way, anointed with the Holy Spirit. Further, the heavenly Father announced for all to hear that this was His Son, the One chosen to fulfill all the promises of the Old Testament (as in Isaiah 42:1). Jesus was the One to bring God's righteousness to sinful humanity (Jeremiah 23:5–6). The appearance of the Holy Spirit was, in particular, the sign God had promised John He would use to identify the Messiah (John 1:32–33).

Second, the anointing of the Holy Spirit strengthened Jesus for the work ahead. Immediately following His baptism, Jesus was led by the Spirit into the wilderness to be tempted by Satan (Matthew 4:1–11). If Jesus was to fulfill all righteousness, that is, to fulfill all the requirements God's Law placed upon humankind (Romans 5:18–19), He would have to defeat the devil's temptations and obey God perfectly. In what sense did Jesus need the strengthening of the Holy Spirit? As true God, of course, Jesus did not need anything from anyone. However, Jesus' mission was not to overwhelm the devil by His omnipotence. It was necessary for Jesus to fulfill as a true man what God demanded of human beings. Therefore He would have to defeat Satan by depending on the Father and using those means God makes available to humankind. Truly, then, at His baptism, Jesus' human nature received a special outpouring of the Holy Spirit (Acts 10:38).

Third, but most important, by being baptized Jesus was putting Himself in the place of all those who did need Baptism for the forgiveness of their sins—the whole human race. Though He had no sin, Jesus became sin so that we could receive His righteousness (2 Corinthians 5:21). When Jesus sacrificed Himself on the cross, then, the payment would be credited to all people.

As Jesus was coming up out of the water the heavens were opened, the Holy Spirit came down upon Jesus in the form of a dove, and God the Father spoke from heaven. This incident is one of the clearest witnesses to the Trinity anywhere in Scripture. The dove recalls the Spirit of God brooding upon the waters at creation (Genesis 1:2), as well as the dove which brought a sign of peace between God and man after the Flood (Genesis 8:8–12). The voice was unmistakably of God, as on two other significant occasions (Matthew 17:5; John 12:2–29). And Jesus was specifically identified as His Son. While the Bible never uses the terms Trinity or tri-une God, here as elsewhere the doctrine of three persons in one God is clearly taught. (See also Genesis 1:26–27: "Let us make man"; Isaiah 48:16: "Sovereign LORD ... Me ... His Spirit;" Matthew 28:19: "the Father and the Son and the Holy Spirit.")

Discussing the Text

1. Why did Jesus wish to be baptized? Why didn't John at first understand?

2. How did God give His public seal of approval to Jesus at His baptism? What does this seal of approval mean for us? See Hebrews 9:26b–28.

3. Why did Jesus need the strengthening of the Holy Spirit for the work ahead? See also Hebrews 4:15.

4. How did Jesus put Himself in the place of all those who needed Baptism when He was baptized? Why is this significant for sinners? See 2 Corinthians 5:21 and Hebrews 2:14–18.

5. How is the Trinity revealed at the baptism of Jesus?

Apply

"This is My Son, whom I love; with Him I am well-pleased" (Matthew 3:17). Besides pointing to Jesus as the Messiah (cf. Psalm 2:7), these words carry tremendous comfort for us. Jesus, after all, has just placed Himself in unity with all sinful people by accepting Baptism. He stands before God as the representative of us all, and He stands there robed in our sin. It is as if Jesus were the greatest of sinners, since the Lord laid on Him the iniquity of us all.

The Father is well-pleased with His Son because Jesus willingly assumed this terrible guilt on our behalf. And God is well-pleased with the way His Son is carrying out His mission—the salvation of all people. Because Jesus did carry out that mission all the way to the cross and the empty tomb, we can have forgiveness and His righteousness.

In Jesus' baptism, as in our own, we may see the most comforting assurance: that God accepts us, is even pleased with us, because He is well-pleased with our Savior. Already we may imagine that someday we will hear God's voice calling us His beloved children.

1. Why do the words, "This is My Son, whom I love; with Him I am well-pleased" provide believers comfort?

2. Why was the Father well-pleased with His Son? How did Jesus' action that was pleasing to God make us pleasing to God (1 Peter 2:24)? Why is this important?

3. Describe how the message revealed in this lesson is comforting to you.

4. In a sense, God has anointed you to be His child. What does that mean to you?

5. God gives you the Holy Spirit to strengthen you for the work He gives you. Why is that important?

6. What important responsibility does God give to parents in Deuteronomy 6:4–9? What are some important tasks God has given you? How do you approach those tasks?

Catechism Connection

Examine Martin Luther's explanation of the blessings of Baptism from the opening for this session.

1. Christ has already won forgiveness and salvation for us. Why, then, do we still need Baptism? See Titus 3:5–7.

2. What connection between faith and Baptism does God reveal in Acts 16:31–33?

Send

To Do This Week

Family Connection

1. Celebrate Baptisms this week. Have a party where you celebrate the forgiveness of sins and the eternal life you received through Holy Baptism.

2. Write each member of your family's baptismal birthday on a calendar. Have a baptismal birthday party on these days.

3. Review the events of today's lesson. Ask, "What does this lesson teach you about Jesus?"

4. Create a family baptismal poster.

Personal Reflection

1. Take out your baptismal certificate. Read it. Meditate on the power and blessings God provided to you at your Baptism.

2. Share with someone the blessings and power you received at your Baptism.

3. Take out Luther's Small Catechism. Review the section on Holy Baptism.

For Next Week

Read John 1:29–41 and Matthew 9:9–13 in preparation for the next session.

Session 7

Jesus Calls Us to Follow Him

(John 1:29–41; Matthew 9:9–13)

——— Gather ———

Theme: Hospital or Museum

Key Point

Jesus' love for us brings about true repentance so that we might live our lives as His disciples.

Objectives

By the power of the Holy Spirit working through God's Word we will

1. describe the men whom Jesus called to be His disciples;
2. explain how the disciples' worthiness to serve as Jesus' disciples came from Jesus' love for them, and not from anything they had done;
3. describe how Jesus continues to call sinners today to be His disciples;
4. affirm Jesus' call to discipleship as a privilege.

Opening

Read together Martin Luther's explanation of Baptism:

Leader: What is Baptism?

Group: Baptism is not just plain water, but it is the water included in God's command and combined with God's word.

Leader: Which is that word of God?

Group: Christ our Lord says in the last chapter of Matthew: "Therefore go and make disciples of all nations, baptizing them in the name of the Father and of the Son and of the Holy Spirit." [Matthew 28:19]

Introduction

"The church is a hospital for sinners, not a museum for saints."
1. Do you agree or disagree with this statement? Why?

2. What danger does a congregation face when it forgets that it is a hospital?

3. How can a congregation continue to act as a hospital rather than becoming a museum?

Study

Examine John 1:29–41 and Matthew 9:9–13.

Reading the Text

To be a disciple of Jesus—one of the original Twelve or one today—always involves a commitment; it is always costly. But discipleship never begins with the disciple; he or she never initiates the relationship with Christ. Today's lessons demonstrate that discipleship is always a privilege to which Christ calls us. It always begins with His grace, His choosing.

Forty days have passed since Jesus' baptism by John. Having turned aside Satan's temptations in the wilderness (Matthew 4:1–11), Jesus now begins His public ministry. Again He visits the messenger whose whole mission is to herald the Christ's arrival, and John does so in most powerful terms: "Behold, the Lamb of God, who takes away the sin of the world!" (John 1:29).

To the first-century Jewish ear, John's announcement could not be more exciting. Immediately would come to mind a seemingly endless procession of sacrifices, going back almost to the beginning of Old Testament history (Genesis 4:4; 22:7–8; Exodus 12:1–14; Isaiah 53:7). Every year there was the Passover lamb. Every day at the temple in Jerusalem a lamb was led to be sacrificed. As Isaiah made clear, each was a symbol of the Messiah, who someday would be led to the slaughter for the sins of the people (Isaiah 53:4–7). It must have seemed, however, that someday would never come. Yet the faithful waited for the One who would actually earn their forgiveness.

Now, suddenly, John was announcing that Jesus was that final, promised Lamb! Somehow God had revealed to John that the visible appearance of the Holy Spirit as a dove was the unmistakable mark of the Savior whose way he had been preparing (John 1:30–34). (John's statement that he did not recognize Jesus probably means he would not have been certain that Jesus was the Messiah apart from this sign.)

Soon two of John's disciples followed Jesus (John 1:35–39). John's repeated exclamation, "Behold!" "Look!", has the force of "That's the One! Follow Him!" (John understood that his followers should not remain with him, but rather become disciples of Jesus; 3:22–30). Jesus' own words are powerful, too. He invites their interest and issues His invitation. "Come and see" (1:39), like "Go and learn" (Matthew 9:13), was an expression among the rabbis indicating that further thought and instruction were necessary. Surely Jesus did a great deal of instructing as the men stayed with Him the rest of that day. From that time on, they were disciples of Christ.

Andrew is remembered as "the Introducer" (see also John 12:20–23). Filled with excitement, he immediately brings to Jesus his brother Simon (1:40–42). Jesus' characterization of Simon as Peter (*Petros* in Greek, *Cephas* in Aramaic), meaning "rock," is prophetic; Peter would come to be strong in faith and a pillar of the early church. Initially, however, Peter was anything but a rock. (In Matthew 16:18 Jesus uses Peter's name as a play on words. The rock upon which the church is built is not Peter, but rather the faith in Christ which he confessed.)

The other disciple who followed Jesus, unnamed in the text, was almost surely John the apostle, author of this gospel. (Compare, for example, John 13:23, 18:15, 20:2, 21:7, 20.) Likely he would have told his brother, James, about Christ. Jesus' core of followers was beginning to take shape.

The core was perhaps completed when Jesus called Matthew (Matthew 9:9), also known as Levi (Mark 2:14; Luke 5:27). It was common in Galilee for men to have two names; for example, Matthew is a Galilean name and Levi a purely Jewish one. Matthew's call is the last to be described in detail. By Matthew 10:1, all 12 disciples are in place. Matthew seems to be emphasizing his own unworthiness for discipleship, as if he could only be an afterthought. (Compare Paul in 1 Corinthians 15:8.)

Matthew was quite right; he was unworthy and particularly so in Jewish eyes. Tax collectors were always viewed by the Jews as evil (Matthew 5:46; 18:17; Luke 18:13) because they collaborated with the Romans in taking money from their own countrymen. Often they were dishonest, for the Roman system allowed them great freedom to assess whatever taxes they could (Luke 3:13; 19:1–10). Matthew was a tax collector of the worst kind—a customs-house official. He had opportunity for greater cheating than common publicans, who only collected regular dues. According to the religious leaders of the day, such "lowest of the low" like Matthew were virtually disqualified from repenting and being saved.

Yet Jesus calls him to repent and believe the Good News. While the rabbis saw repentance as something that people had to do to make themselves acceptable to God, Jesus now makes clear that His act of love brings about true repentance. Jesus makes the move. He goes to Matthew even as Matthew is carrying out his business and says, "Follow Me!" The imperative, or command, to follow Jesus is a statement of Law. But the fact that Jesus spoke to Matthew is Good News—Jesus had accepted Matthew, with all of his sins, as one of His own. Matthew was forgiven.

Working in Capernaum, where men such as Peter and Andrew, James and John paid taxes for their fishing partnership, Matthew had no doubt heard of Jesus. Perhaps he had heard Him preach. Now he did not hesitate. He rose immediately and followed, for Jesus had changed his heart. A changed heart is the essence of true repentance, and only Jesus' love can bring it about.

Not surprisingly, then, Jesus accepted an invitation to

Matthew's house, where other tax collectors and notorious sinners gathered. The Pharisees, of course, were scandalized by such association (Matthew 9:10–13). Jesus had come to save sinners, just as a doctor heals the sick. (Thus it is well said that the church is a hospital for sinners, not a museum for saints!) Jesus understood what the Pharisees had yet to "go and learn": that God prefers mercy (or compassion) for the needy to outward acts of religion ("sacrifice").

Hosea 5:15–6:6 is the "source" for Jesus' teaching. There "mercy" or "compassion" may be better translated as "loyalty," for God is demanding loyalty to Himself. This is a result of His perfect loyalty to, or compassion or mercy toward, sinful people. The comparison of the passages, along with Matthew 12:1–7, seems to give this meaning: because God reaches out to sinners and remains loyal to them despite their sin, sinners are therefore to be faithful to God, which is best expressed in kindness to others in need.

Discussing the Text

1. How does the message of today's lesson contradict the words of the song that begins with the words, "I have decided to follow Jesus."? See John 15:16.

2. What is the significance of John announcing Jesus as the "Lamb of God" (John 1:29, 36)?

3. Share a little information about each of the disciples:
• Andrew (John 1:40–42)

• Peter (John 1:40–42)

• John (John 1:35–40; 18:15)

61

- James (Matthew 17:1)

- Matthew (Matthew 9:9)

4. What makes the call of Matthew to serve as Jesus' disciple so remarkable?

5. Compare the rabbi's view of repentance to Jesus' view of repentance. See Matthew 9:11–13.

Apply

The fact that Christ calls people to be His disciples—rather than people initiating the relationship themselves—implies at least two applications for our lives. First, since Christ calls, we cannot refuse. It is not an option whether a Christian will be an active disciple of Jesus. When we were baptized, we were marked for life-long, committed service to God's kingdom. By God's grace, we will not remain passive, "go through the motions" Christians. We can introduce friends, or even brothers and sisters, to Jesus. We can come and see more of Him in His Word. We can, by the Spirit's power, follow Him wherever He asks us to go.

We need never doubt that we are indeed disciples, though we may feel inadequate to carry out such an honored calling. We need not wonder whether we are really included in the great tasks of sharing Christ. We need not think we are just tagging along behind, unworthy to approach Jesus. Jesus has turned to us, invited us to walk and work with Him. This assurance our Baptism also gives. Since Jesus has forgiven our sins, given us life with Him forever, He certainly will enable us to do the things He asks of disciples.

1. What is the significance that Jesus has called us to be His disciples, rather than we deciding to be Jesus' disciples? What further assurance do we find in Romans 8:30?

2. What assurance does our Baptism provide concerning our discipleship?

3. How does the assurance of the forgiveness of sins and eternal life motivate us to serve as Jesus' disciples? See 1 John 4:19.

4. Complete the following sentence starter: Discipleship is …

5. Discuss ways members of your group carry out Jesus' directive, "Follow Me," individually and as a congregation. What is one change you would like to make in your commitment?

Catechism Connection

Examine Martin Luther's explanation of Baptism from the opening for this session. Also read 1 Peter 3:18–21.

1. Compare the water of Baptism with the water of the Great Flood.

2. How are we saved by Christ's death (verse 18)? How are we saved by His resurrection (verse 21; see also 1 Corinthians 15:14)?

3. How does Baptism lead to a good conscience (verse 21)?

Send

To Do This Week

Family Connection

1. Review the calling of Jesus' disciples. Ask, "Who did the calling in each of the events?"

2. Say, "God called each of us to be His disciples through Holy Baptism." Ask, "What does it mean to be Jesus' disciples?"

3. Make a list of ways you might better serve as Jesus' disciples.

4. Write "We are Jesus' disciples" on a note card. Place the card in a conspicuous place, where everyone in the family will read it often.

Personal Reflection

1. List the ways you can demonstrate that you have been chosen by Jesus as one of His disciples.

2. Consider the significance of the fact that Jesus chose us to be His disciples. We did nothing to earn or to deserve the role of disciple.

3. Disciples learn. Consider opportunities to study God's Word this week. Disciples serve. Consider opportunities to share God's love with others this week.

For Next Week

Read Matthew 18:21–35; Mark 10:13–16; and 1 Corinthians 1:10–17 in preparation for the next class session.

Session 8

Jesus Helps Us Love and Forgive One Another

(Matthew 18:21–35; Mark 10:13–16; 1 Corinthians 1:10–17)

Gather

Theme: How Many Times?

Key Point

God's great love for us motivates and empowers us to forgive others.

Objectives

By the power of the Holy Spirit working through God's Word we will

1. confess our unwillingness to forgive those who sin against us;
2. explain God's attitude toward forgiveness—His forgiveness for our sins through Christ and His desire for us to forgive others;
3. affirm that Jesus won forgiveness for all people through His death on the cross;
4. forgive others who have sinned against us.

Opening

Read the Fifth Petition of the Lord's Prayer and Martin Luther's explanation:

Group: And forgive us our trespasses as we forgive those who trespass against us.

Leader: What does this mean?

Group: We pray in this petition that our Father in heaven would not look at our sins, or deny our prayer because of them. We are neither worthy of the things for which we pray, nor have we deserved them, but we ask that He would give them all to us by grace, for we daily sin much and surely deserve nothing but punishment. So we too will sincerely forgive and gladly do good to those who sin against us.

Introduction

"How many times must I forgive someone who continually sins against me?"

1. How do many people answer this question? What does a person's response to this question tell you about them?

2. How have you answered this question? What does your response to the question tell you about yourself?

3. How does God answer the question? What does His response to the question tell you about Him?

In today's lesson we witness the great love God has for all people. We hear Jesus teach about forgiveness—His forgiveness for us and our forgiveness of others.

Study

Examine Matthew 18:21–25; Mark 10:13–16; and 1 Corinthians 1:10–17.

Reading the Text

Whoever we are, whatever we've done, at whatever age, Jesus stands with open arms to embrace us. In today's lessons, He shows His limitless love and patience for all people and teaches His disciples to welcome—or welcome back—their fellow disciples.

The parable of the unforgiving servant follows immediately after the well-known passage on restoring Christians who have strayed (Matthew 18:12–20). The church is to work tirelessly, Jesus says, to bring sinful members back into the fold by repentance and forgiveness. Peter thinks He grasps this teaching of Christ, so he tests his understanding (18:21). According to rabbinic practice, a repeat sinner was to be forgiven no more than three times. Peter, however, senses that Jesus wishes to be even more generous. Should he forgive perhaps seven times?

"Not seven times, but seventy times seven!" (18:22). Forgiveness is never to be numbered. When it seems enough has been given (the number *seven* often symbolizes completeness), it is to be multiplied further. (The alternate translation, "seventy-seven times," conveys the same point.) Forgiving others is to be limitless because Christ never stops forgiving us. He forgives not just sins (which might be counted), but sin (the total condition of human beings which makes them guilty continually).

To illustrate the point, Jesus tells the parable (18:23–35). The imagery suggests a king calling to account various governors and regional officials under him. One of these, in administering his territories, has accumulated such an absurdly large debt that it could never be repaid. (Ten thousand talents may equate to anywhere from $10 million to many times that in today's money.) In such cases, the king was legally justified in selling the man and his family into slavery (Exodus 22:3; 2 Kings 4:1). The proceeds would then cover at least a small portion of the debt.

The king knows that the servant's plea for more time is useless. Nevertheless, he has mercy and forgives him the entire debt; not only will he not be punished, but he no longer has to repay. This, of course, is precisely what God has done for us. Our sin is a debt we could never repay, but God canceled it because Jesus paid all by His death. God's forgiveness is not just a matter of overlooking sin, but rather of paying its incredible price Himself.

The servant, one thinks, will surely be merciful to anyone who owes him anything. It is truly shocking, therefore, when he violently demands payment for a trifling debt. (A denarius was a working man's daily wage, so 100 denarii was a sum which could be paid back.) The servant actually goes out looking for his debtor and grabs him by the throat (the full extent of force which Roman law permitted a creditor). Though the man begs precisely the same mercy the first servant had asked of the king, the wicked servant casts his fellow servant into prison.

Now the point of the parable: when the king hears of the servant's ruthlessness, his patience becomes passionate anger. He condemns the servant's lovelessness, and he has him delivered to the torturers—from whom he will never be released. "This," Jesus says, "is how My heavenly Father will treat each of you unless you forgive your brother from your heart" (18:35).

The conclusion of the parable is chilling. Anyone who refuses to forgive will suffer eternally. It should be kept in mind, though, that the basis for our forgiving one another is the immeasurable forgiveness God has given us in Christ.

In stark contrast to the loveless servant in the parable, Jesus' blessing the children (Mark 10:13–16) is surely one of the most attractive stories of His entire ministry. Here, too, however, Christ's love is a vivid counterpoint to the disciples' thoughtlessness.

Only shortly before, Jesus had spoken of receiving a child as a precious little one who believes in Him (9:36–37, 42). Now children are brought to Jesus for a blessing, likely by their mothers. The children were of all ages, but certainly included the tiniest babies. (Luke's account uses the Greek word *brephos*, which specifies infants and even unborn children [Luke 18:15]. Mark and Matthew use the word *paidion*, which includes both infants and slightly older children.)

According to Jewish tradition, spending time with small children was beneath the dignity of a rabbi. Perhaps for that reason the disciples try to keep them away from Jesus. Jesus will have none of it. He is "indignant" with the disciples. (This is the only occasion in the New Testament that this very strong word for anger is used of Jesus.) Jesus loves the little children. He welcomes them, takes them in His arms, and blesses them.

Jesus, of course, welcomes everyone. But His reason in this case is special. Children, He says, are the model citizens of God's kingdom (Mark 10:14). Theirs is the ideal faith, because their reason does not yet raise doubts as it does in adults. Children trust implicitly whomever provides for their needs, while adults are always tempted—in fact, taught—to be self-reliant. As Jesus touched these little ones, they believed in Him. And for anyone of any age to be saved, he must believe as these did (10:15).

Discussing the Text

1. What indication does Peter provide that he doesn't understand the essence of the parable (Matthew 18:21)?

2. What is the significance of Jesus' response to Peter, "Not seven times, but seventy times seven!"? See also Job 5:19 and Proverbs 24:16.

3. Compare the king's mercy and forgiveness demonstrated to the servant to the mercy and forgiveness Jesus has provided and continues to provide to us.

4. In response to the great love and mercy Jesus demonstrated by paying the debt for our sins on the cross, how does God desire that we treat a brother or sister who has sinned against us?

5. How does Jesus' blessing the children stand in stark contrast to the loveless servant in the parable? Considering Jewish tradition, why are Jesus' actions so remarkable?

6. Review 1 Corinthians 1:10–17. What kinds of problems resulted when these early Christians failed to follow Jesus' command to forgive one another? What model for unity does Paul give?

Apply

First, the parable of the unforgiving servant emphasizes that God has forgiven us more than we can ever measure. That is the supreme comfort. No matter how unfaithful we have been, God still wipes our records clean. This forgiveness, we know, is for the sake of Jesus' death and resurrection.

On the other hand, the failures to embrace others—whether fellow sinners or little children—are stern warnings to us. Both biblical incidents were met with the strongest reprimands. It is vital that we learn to forgive as we have been forgiven and welcome to Christ as we have been welcomed by Christ.

1. Describe the comfort you have in knowing that God has forgiven you through the death of His only Son on the cross.

2. How does confessing to God that you are the chief of sinners for whom Jesus died, and knowing that you are forgiven for His sake, motivate you to forgive others?

3. How does God desire that we treat all people? How will this treatment provide us the opportunity to share our faith in Jesus?

4. Create a prayer giving thanks for the forgiveness Jesus won for you on the cross. Pray that by the power of the Holy Spirit you would be motivated by Jesus' love to forgive others. Plan to share the prayer with your family and read it daily during the next week.

5. Evaluate whether it's better to say, "That's okay" or "I forgive you" after someone apologizes to you.

6. Talk about times when it may be especially difficult for Christians to forgive others. How can Peter's advice in 1 Peter 4:11 help us in those situations?

Catechism Connection

Review the Fifth Petition of the Lord's Prayer and Martin Luther's explanation from the opening for this session.

1. Read Matthew 6:9–15. How does Jesus emphasize the importance of the Fifth Petition?

2. Read Psalm 51:1–2 and Psalm 130:3–4. When might these verses be especially meaningful to a Christian?

3. Read Ephesians 4:32. How does God's mercy change us?

Send

To Do This Week

Family Connection

1. Review the parable of the unmerciful servant. Discuss the significance of the debt that was paid in full by the merciful king. Then compare the parable to the debt that Jesus paid for you on the cross.

2. Role-play saying, "I forgive you," when a family member apologizes. Encourage one another to put this procedure into practice.

3. Pray together the prayer written in "Apply."

4. Discuss times when it is hard to forgive someone. Then consider people whom you or other members of your family have not forgiven. Make it a point this week to forgive those people.

Personal Reflection

1. Confess your unwillingness to forgive like Jesus. Then consider the fact that Jesus went to the cross to suffer and die for all of your sins. Pray that the Holy Spirit would empower you through Jesus' love to forgive others.

2. Reread stanza 1 of "Chief of Sinners though I Be." Meditate on the significance of the words.

For Next Week

Read Matthew 5:1–12 and 14:22–33 in preparation for the next session.

Session 9

Jesus Teaches His Disciples to Trust Him

(Matthew 5:1–12; 14:22–33)

Gather

Theme: "Trust Me"

Key Point

God's love for us enables us to turn to Him at all times, as we echo the words "Lord save us," knowing that nothing can or will separate us from His love.

Objectives

By the power of the Holy Spirit working through God's Word we will

1. explain how each of the Beatitudes describes the blessings we have received through faith in Christ Jesus;
2. confess the lack of trust we often demonstrate as we face trials, hardships, and persecutions;
3. affirm the love that Jesus demonstrated to His disciples as they faced the storm along with the love He provides us as we face storms in our lives;
4. face storms in life with confidence and hope.

Opening

Read the First Commandment and Martin Luther's explanation.

All: You shall have no other gods.

Leader: What does this mean?

All: We should fear, love, and trust in God above all things.

Introduction

"Trust me!"

1. When have you or someone you know spoken these words? Describe the situation.

2. Why is it often difficult to trust others even when they say, "Trust me"?

In today's lesson, we will explore the results of trust in Jesus. As we do so, we will be reminded that God in His love for us in Jesus is completely trustworthy. We can rely on Him to help us as we face difficulties in life and as we seek His forgiveness for our sinful thoughts, words, and actions.

Study

Examine Matthew 5:1–12 and 14:22–33.

Reading the Text

For both the day-to-day stresses and crises of life, Jesus says, "Trust Me." By gentle teaching and by dramatic action, the Savior leads His disciples to a deeper faith in Him.

The Beatitudes (Matthew 5:1–12) are some of the Bible's most comforting expressions of God's blessing, particularly as His people face adversity. In eight beautiful pearls, Jesus assures believers that they are blessed, even when circumstances seem to imply otherwise. The Beatitudes (from a Latin word meaning "supreme blessedness or happiness") are both Law and Gospel. Unfortunately, they are often misunderstood and taught as Law—something hearers are to do in order to become Jesus' disciples. These words are spoken to those who already are supremely blessed by Him who has called them, all unworthy, to be His disciples. That is the good news. At the same time, the Beatitudes remind us of what should be a description of the Christian life, and in that they show us how much room there is in us for growth. We are constantly to become in our lives more of what, by God's grace, we already are—the children of God.

Jesus sits down, probably on a hillside overlooking a broad plain (compare Luke 6:12, 17–23) and begins to teach (Matthew 5:1–2). One can imagine both the gentle manner of His voice and the sense of comfort His hearers must have felt. Each Beatitude begins with a form of the Greek word *makarios*("blessed" or "happy"). *Makarios* usually describes not a blessing being given, but rather a blessed condition which already exists. Jesus' point is that the people He is describing are blessed— already.

So who are these people, and how are they blessed? Simply put, they are all people who believe in Christ. Jesus is saying that the believer inside each Christian actually fits the following description and is blessed in the following ways.

Christians ...
5:3 are poor in spirit (realize they are beggars before God)
5:4 mourn over their guilt and the tragic effects of sin
5:5 are meek (patient, trusting that God will vindicate them)
5:6 hunger and thirst for righteousness (i.e., forgiveness)
5:7 are merciful (caring for fellow human beings in need)
5:8 are pure in heart (fully devoted to obey and praise God)
5:9 are peacemakers, as Christ restored their peace with God
5:10 are persecuted, just as the prophets were

and they are blessed in that God ...
• has given them His kingdom, both now and forever
• comforts them with the presence of Christ
• gives them the earth (All things are in fact theirs!)
• fills them with forgiveness for Jesus' sake
• shows them mercy by relieving their suffering
• will let them see Him face to face in heaven
• will call them His sons, after His beloved Son
• assures them again of their place in His kingdom

Faith in Jesus will, naturally and spontaneously, bear fruit in these actions by the believer, and God's blessings always come through faith alone. In truth, Jesus Himself is the One who has done all the begging (5:3), mourning (5:4), waiting and trusting (5:5), peacemaking (5:9), and all the rest completely for His people.

Jesus gave His disciples a more dramatic lesson in faith on the Sea of Galilee (Matthew 14:22–33). Really a lake, just 13 miles long and 6 miles wide, the "sea" is nevertheless known for its sudden and dangerous storms. (See also 8:23–27 and Lesson 12). Surrounding mountains tend to funnel the wind, causing violent waves that can be deadly to fishermen today.

Having just fed the 5,000 (14:13–21), Jesus was alone that night praying when His disciples were caught in such a storm. It was very late; the fourth watch was 3–6 A.M.). Far from land (3 to 3½ miles, John 6:19), and frightened by the storm, the disciples are terrified by the figure approaching across the water.

Jesus' answer, "Take courage! It is I" (14:27), meant much more than just, "Don't be afraid—it's not a ghost." This was a complete assurance against all fear. With Jesus present, the disciples needed nothing else.

Peter believed. Peter knew that Jesus could enable even such a miracle as letting him walk on water, too. Trusting Jesus' invitation (14:29), he stepped out of the boat. Only when he doubted, following his senses rather than Jesus' word, did Peter begin to sink.

Jesus reproves Peter for his "little faith." Yet in those very words, Jesus acknowledges that Peter does have faith. The most important expression of it, perhaps, was his desperate cry, "Lord, save me!" This is the ultimate plea of every believer. And as Jesus immediately reached out to Peter, so He always answers with salvation everyone else who cries out.

No sooner do Jesus and Peter come aboard, than the storm ceases. (John's account seems to imply also that the boat was suddenly, miraculously, at shore, John 6:21.) It has been a powerful faith-building experience for the disciples. After an earlier storm at sea, they had asked in amazement, "What kind of man is this?" (Matthew 8:27) Now they answer their own question: "Truly You are the Son of God!" (14:33). This marks the moment as one of the high points of Matthew's gospel.

Discussing the Text

1. How are the Beatitudes (Matthew 5:3–12) a source of comfort for God's people, particularly as they face troubles, hardships, and persecution?

2. Look again at the descriptions of Christians and ways we are blessed on page 75. Which of the blessings are especially meaningful to you? Why?

3. How are the Beatitudes often misunderstood and taught as Law? How does this improper teaching rob the Beatitudes of comfort and hope?

4. How is the blessing Jesus teaches not a blessing being given, but a blessing that exists? How did God provide this blessing to us?

5. Why might one expect the reaction of the disciples when they were caught in the storm (Matthew 14:22–26)?

6. How are Jesus' words to Peter, "You of little faith" (verse 31), both a reproof and a comfort to Peter?

7. How was Peter's cry for help (verse 30) the same cry we make as we confess our sins?

8. How was the disciples' response to Jesus' miracle similar to the way we respond to the miracle of forgiveness of sins and eternal life that Jesus has accomplished for us?

Apply

Whether facing imminent danger or just daily discouragement, we need to know that Jesus is always present to bless and protect us. Sometimes—in an automobile accident or on a dark street—we may be terrified to the point of crying out, "Lord, save me!" More often, being humble, meek, kind, pure, peace-loving will earn us persecution and ridicule. God's promises give courage to His children in such troublesome moments.

For that reason, it is crucial that in these lessons Christ's loving work be emphasized, rather than turning them into instructions in how we are to be. An appropriate application of the Beatitudes is not, for example, "So, see, you should go and make peace with your friends." More faithful to Jesus' words would be something like, "Being a Christian may not seem very macho because it means being meek instead of tough, but that's okay because God really gives us everything we could ever want."

Likewise, the primary lesson of Jesus' coming to the disciples on the water is not, "Your faith is so small. You ought to trust Jesus more." Instead, Jesus is saying to us, "You can always call on Me. I'll always be there to lift you up!"

1. What encouragement do both of the accounts studied today provide us as we face hardships, temptations, persecutions, etc.?

2. How would focusing on our actions destroy the crucial lessons provided in both accounts?

3. Even as Peter's faith was small, Jesus aggressively pulled Peter out of the sea—saved Him from certain death. Compare this event to your own life. How does Jesus' action on Peter's behalf provide comfort?

4. When asked, "How are you?" some people reply, "I'm blessed." What does such a reply suggest about a person? How might others react to that answer?

5. Compare "godliness with contentment" (1 Timothy 6:6–8) with the Beatitudes.

Catechism Connection

Review the First Commandment and Martin Luther's explanation from the opening for this session.

1. Read Mark 12:28–34. Describe the love God requires (verses 30–31).

2. Why shouldn't this requirement lead to hopelessness? See 2 Corinthians 5:21.

3. The teacher seemed to understand God's law of love (Mark 12:32–34). What else was necessary?

Send

To Do This Week

Family Connection

1. Use the Beatitudes in your daily devotions. Read them aloud together or responsively. Remind your children that the blessings Jesus teaches about He earned for them on the cross.

2. Review the story of the stilling of the storm. At times we may face storms in our lives. How can Jesus' love for us comfort us and equip us to face these storms?

3. Share with each other people who may be facing storms in their lives. Pray for these people. Share with them in person, on the phone, or in a card that you are praying for them.

4. Practice answering "I'm blessed" to the question, "How are you?" Begin using that response in your family this week. Consider making it a normal response.

Personal Reflection

1. Meditate on a different Beatitude each day this week. Consider how Jesus has provided you the blessing through His death on the cross.

2. Befriend a person who is facing a storm in his/her life.

For Next Week

Read Matthew 17:1–9 in preparation for the next session.

Session 10

Jesus Shows His Glory

(Matthew 17:1–9)

Gather

Theme: Ah Hah!

Key Point

We rejoice in Jesus' victory over sin and death, for by God's grace, through faith, His victory becomes ours.

Objectives

By the power of the Holy Spirit working through God's Word we will
1. list the events of the Transfiguration;
2. describe the significance of the Transfiguration for the disciples and us;
3. confess our hopeless sinful condition;
4. witness boldly the glory of God as revealed in the person and work of Jesus.

Opening

Sing or speak together the following stanzas of "How Good, Lord, to Be Here."

How good, Lord, to be here!
Your glory fills the night;
Your face and garments, like the sun,
Shine with unborrowed light.

How good, Lord, to be here,
Your beauty to behold
Where Moses and Elijah stand,
Your messengers of old.

> Before we taste of death,
> We see Your kingdom come;
> We long to hold the vision bright
> And make this hill our home.
>
> How good, Lord, to be here!
> Yet we may not remain;
> But since You bid us leave the mount,
> Come with us to the plain.

Introduction

"Ah Hah!"

1. When have you or someone you know exclaimed, "Ah hah," as you have had a new insight or understanding?

2. How can the knowledge of the person and work of Jesus on your behalf become an "ah hah" experience?

Today three of Jesus' disciples have an "ah hah" experience as they witness the Transfiguration of Jesus. To them Jesus reveals who He is and the purpose for which He came. Through His Word, God continues to reveal who Jesus is and the purpose for which He came so that all people might exclaim "ah hah" through the gift of faith.

Study

Examine Matthew 17:1–9.

Reading the Text

The Transfiguration is the climax of Christ's epiphany, His revealing or "shining upon" the nations. It fortifies the disciples for the faith-shaking events ahead, Jesus' suffering and death. For our lives as Christians, the transfiguration of Jesus shows His glory in our midst.

Just six days before, Peter had declared Jesus to be the Christ, an "epiphany" specifically revealed to him by the heavenly Father (Matthew 16:16–17). What the disciples did not yet realize was that the Christ was destined to go to the cross to suffer and die for the world's sins. Moreover, the Christ's followers would bear crosses, too (16:21–26). This, when it happened, would certainly throw the disciples into confusion. So Jesus grants His closest followers a glimpse of His divine majesty.

Peter, James, and John are chosen to accompany Jesus "up a high mountain." It was, perhaps, the end of a Sabbath, with the sun setting. Jesus led the disciples to one of the slopes around Mount Hermon, the snow-covered peak that commands a view of all Palestine from the north. They were quite alone.

Suddenly, as Jesus was praying (Luke 9:29), He was transfigured before their eyes. "Transfigured" (from the Greek root of our word *metamorphosis*) literally means to be transformed, changed in form. The three Gospel accounts describe Christ's appearance as shining "like the sun," "white as light" (Matthew 17:2), "bright as a flash of lightning" (Luke 9:29), and "dazzling white, whiter than anyone in the world could bleach them" (Mark 9:3).

Two of the Old Testament's greatest heroes, Moses and Elijah, were standing and speaking with Jesus (Matthew 17:3). Both had gone to heaven centuries before, Moses by death (though God had buried him, no one knew the location of his grave, [Deuteronomy 34:6]), and Elijah without ever dying (2 Kings 2:11–12). Yet the disciples were immediately able to recognize them.

Moses and Elijah represent the entire Old Testament. The Jews often referred to their scriptures as "the Law and the Prophets" (Matthew 7:12; 22:40). The *Law*, in this usage, was the first five books of the Bible, authored by Moses. The title *Prophets* summarized the remainder. Elijah was remembered, with Moses, as the greatest of the ancient prophets, and the two of them were pictured together at the close of the Old Testament (Malachi 4:4–6).

What were Jesus, Moses, and Elijah talking about? They spoke of Jesus' "departure" (in Greek, His "exodus"), which He was to accomplish soon in Jerusalem (Luke 9:31). Jesus was on His way to Jerusalem to die, to rise, and to ascend back to heaven. Tragic though the coming events would initially seem, they would indeed be like the exodus of old; they would deliver God's people out of bondage into the freedom of eternal life.

Jesus' departure, of course, was the whole point of His coming, and preparation for it was the point of the Transfiguration. But Peter, James, and John missed the point. Stumbling for words (Mark 9:6), Peter suggested that he and his friends build shelters for the more illustrious three so that they could all remain in the moment permanently (Matthew 17:4). Obviously Peter misunderstood the necessity of Jesus' moving on from glory here to suffering below. He also still failed to grasp the uniqueness of Christ, since he wanted to build three equal or similar shelters.

That would now be corrected. From a bright cloud, God the Father announced: "This one, Jesus, is My beloved Son, with whom I am well-pleased. Listen to Him!" (17:5) Moses, Elijah, and Jesus were not to be viewed equally. Jesus was the completion, the fulfillment, of everything for which Moses and Elijah had been sent. He is not just another prophet; He is the one and only Son of God, the Savior.

The disciples fell on their faces in terror (17:6). Not only was the voice of the Father overwhelming, but even the message was frightening. The man who had walked with them for nearly three years was so much more than they understood. Had they appreciated Him enough? Could they bear to be near Him anymore? Not this way! As never before Peter, James, and John felt the immensity of difference between themselves and the Lord.

Then Jesus reached out and touched them (17:7–8). His words were comforting and His appearance again comfortable, the one they had always known. He was still their Jesus, their friend. Yes, they could continue to walk with Him.

But they had a wonderful new insight. The One so familiar, so friendly, was also so mighty, so glorious. The new understanding would not make full sense to them or to anyone else until after Jesus' resurrection (17:9), because Christ's death, not His glory, was the purpose of His mission. But it was an image the disciples could ponder in the days ahead when all would seem lost. And in the years to follow, it would serve as a powerful reinforcement that their faith in Christ was rightly placed (2 Peter 1:16–19).

Discussing the Text

1. How is the Transfiguration the climax of Jesus' epiphany?

2. Why do you think Jesus selected Peter, James, and John to accompany Him up the mountain? What insights do you find in Acts 3:11–16 and 12:1–4?

3. What would it mean to the disciples to see Jesus transfigured (Matthew 17:2)?

4. Compare Matthew 17:5 with 3:17. What impact would the Father's words have on Peter, James, and John?

5. What do Moses and Elijah represent? How is their presence significant?

6. What does Peter's desire to build three shelters tell us about His understanding of the person and work of Jesus? Of who Jesus was?

7. What new insight did the disciples receive through their experience?

Apply

The relevance of the Transfiguration for us parallels the meaning Jesus intended for Peter, James, and John.

It provides encouragement for us when we feel down. Jesus appears in His shining glory. He is truly the Son of God, the Lord who possesses all authority and power. When circumstances seem hopeless, He is our hope. We may always go on in confidence, because the One who is walking with us is the all-glorious Christ.

The Transfiguration also gives us, like the disciples, a glimpse of our own glory to come. In the Resurrection, our own bodies will be transformed to be like Christ's glorious body (Philippians 3:21), shining like the sun (Daniel 12:3). As Moses and Elijah appeared again alive, so we will live forever in the radiant presence of Christ. This, too, is the hope to sustain us in hard times.

1. How is the Transfiguration relevant for you today?

2. How does the Transfiguration give us a glimpse into the glory we will receive and experience when we leave this life on earth and enter into eternal life?

3. How does the promise of our eternal life give us comfort, hope, and encouragement as we face day-to-day struggles?

4. We may wish we had the opportunity to witness Jesus' glory. Read 2 Corinthians 12:1–10. What did Paul learn was most important for him in this life? Why is this true for us, also?

Catechism Connection

Review the Second Article of the Apostles' Creed in the opening for Session 2.

1. Peter, James, and John saw a glimpse of Jesus' state of exaltation. Which words of the Second Article describe that state?

2. Paul describes Christ's states of humiliation and exaltation in Philippians 2:6–11. What reason does Paul give for Christ's exaltation?

3. Read Romans 8:34. What blessing do we receive from Christ in His exalted state?

Send

To Do This Week

Family Connection

1. Create a family poster and/or mural to show the events of the Transfiguration.

2. Spend time together talking about the significance of the Transfiguration for our lives today. At the end of the discussion have each family member complete this sentence starter, "Because of Jesus' transfiguration I …"

3. Create a Transfiguration card to send to a friend or loved one. On the card share the reason for the hope you have everyday.

Personal Reflection

1. Thank God for revealing His love and forgiveness for you through the person and work of Jesus.

2. Consider how when we enter heaven we too will be transformed to be like Christ's glorious body.

3. Ponder the words of the hymn "How Good, Lord, to Be Here."

For Next Week

Read Matthew 4:1–11 and 8:23–27 in preparation for the next session.

Session 11

Jesus Shows His Power

(Matthew 4:1–11; 8:23–27)

Gather

Theme: Power!

Key Point

The victory Jesus proclaimed over sin, death, and the power of the devil when He rose from the dead becomes *our* victory over sin, death, and the power of the devil by God's grace through faith.

Objectives

By the power of the Holy Spirit working through God's Word we will
1. describe the temptations Jesus faced in the desert and His response to each;
2. confess that we often give in to temptation and sin;
3. rejoice in the fact that Jesus fulfilled perfectly the Law on our behalf and then suffered and died on the cross to win for us forgiveness for our inability to keep the Law;
4. seek new opportunities to strengthen our faith by the power of the Holy Spirit working through the Word of God so that we too may resist temptation.

Opening

Read the Seventh Petition of the Lord's Prayer and Martin Luther's explanation responsively:

All: But deliver us from evil.

Leader: What does this mean?

Group: We pray in this petition, in summary, that our Father in heaven would rescue us from every evil of body and soul,

> possessions and reputation, and finally, when our last hour comes, give us a blessed end, and graciously take us from this valley of sorrow to Himself in heaven.

Introduction

1. List the characteristics of someone who is powerless.

2. List the characteristics of someone who has power.

3. How does a person receive power?

In today's lesson we witness Jesus tempted by Satan in the desert. Jesus responds to those temptations with the power of God's Word. God continues to provide power today through His Word. The Holy Spirit working through God's Word strengthens our faith, empowering us to resist the devil's temptations and to trust God for help in all situations we may encounter.

Study

Examine Matthew 4:1–11 and 8:23–27.

Reading the Text

Matthew 4:1–11. Ever since the Garden of Eden, both humankind and creation itself have been suffering the effects of sin. Human beings die as a result of their sin. Storms and natural violence wreak destruction. (Though commonly called "acts of God," they are really the result of sin.) Today's lessons show, however, that

Jesus Christ, as true man and true God, has undone the corruption of sin and prepared for the restoration of all things.

Jesus was anointed with the Holy Spirit at His baptism (Matthew 3:16–17; see commentary on Lesson 6). Now the Spirit leads Him into the desert, specifically to be tempted by the devil (Matthew 4:1). More than that, the Spirit "impelled" Him or "drove" Him into the wilderness. What was about to happen in the desert becomes an integral part of Jesus' mission on earth.

Jesus' suffering and death were, of course, necessary for the salvation of the world. But just as necessary was His perfect keeping of God's Law, His "active obedience." (Christ's suffering and death is referred to as His "passive obedience," for He obeyed God's will by allowing—passively—His enemies to kill Him.) God's Law was serious and binding, never abolished, and it had to be kept (Matthew 5:17, 48). Just as He had come to pay on the cross for our failures to obey, so also Jesus had come to obey for us (Romans 5:18–19).

Satan, therefore, takes aim at Christ at the beginning of His public ministry. Just one sin by Jesus, and no one would be left to fulfill the demands of God's Law. Every soul would be lost to hell.

The three temptations epitomize all of the devil's temptations to human beings: the desires for material things (Matthew 4:2–4), for popularity (4:5–7), and for power (4:8–10). Yet as Satan brought these temptations against Jesus, much more was involved. Already the possessor of all wealth, fame, and power, Jesus could not be allured so easily. The temptations Jesus faced were instead a challenge to His unique role as the Messiah.

The devil's first statement, for example (4:2–3), tempted Jesus to doubt His heavenly Father's providing: "If you are the Son of God, tell these stones to become bread." (Notice in all three temptations the uncertainties the devil offers: the repeated use of the conditional *if*. By contrast, God gives solid assurances in Holy Scripture.) As a real man, Jesus was surely hungry after 40 days, and as God's Son He could easily have remedied the need. But as Messiah, Jesus trusted the Father for all things—many of them much more important than bread. After all, God's Word provides everything one needs, Jesus says (4:4; see Deuteronomy 8:3).

In the second temptation, the devil suggests to Jesus an easy way to fulfill His destiny as Messiah (4:5–6). Jewish tradition held that when the Messiah came, He would appear on the pinnacle of the temple to summon the faithful. Every morning, a priest would blow a trumpet from that spot, and throngs of worshipers would gather. Doing what Satan suggested, leaping 15 stories and landing safely in the courtyard below the crowds, would immediately have acclaimed Jesus as the Promised One. He would have become immensely popular—a much easier way to be the Messiah than by going to the cross! This time the devil even quotes Scripture—out of context—to support his case (Psalm 91:11–12). Again, however, Jesus turns aside the temptation by turning to God's Word in Deuteronomy 6:16 (Matthew 4:7).

Third, the devil offers Jesus all the kingdoms of the world for one "small" act of worship (4:8–9). This offer was real. Evil does rule in this sinful world, and Satan would have stepped aside and given Jesus free reign, because Satan would then have succeeded in his great ambition—to be God's god. Jesus understood, though, that the Messiah was not to gain the kingdoms of the world. He had come to establish the kingdom of heaven (4:17). It would be an awful fate to remain forever in the kingdoms of this world, corrupt as they are, but Christ's mission was to deliver His people from them.

Jesus' command that Satan be "away!" effectively put a stop to this round of temptation. Worship belongs only to the Lord God (4:10; Deuteronomy 6:13). Defeated, Satan retreats, to try again at another time (Luke 4:13). Angels came and ministered to Jesus (Matthew 4:11). God does provide the help for which Jesus had trusted Him!

Could Jesus have failed in His struggle with the devil? No, since Jesus' will is that of the Father (John 5:30; 6:38; 10:30), Christ was incapable of sinning. Nevertheless, the temptations—and the struggle against them—were very real and the victory over them absolutely necessary.

Matthew 8:23–27. One of the results of sin has been the disharmony of nature (Genesis 3:17–19), including storms at sea (Matthew 8:23–27). Several of Jesus' disciples were experienced sailors, but they knew the dangers of sudden squalls on the Sea of Galilee. (See commentary on Lesson 9.) What they did not yet understand was that their Master was also master of the wind and the waves.

The day had been busy. It was probably the day on which Jesus spoke His many "parables of the kingdom" (Mark 4:1–35). Exhausted, Jesus instructed the disciples to ferry over to the other side of the lake, while He lay down in the stern to sleep (Mark 4:38). As the storm began to howl and waves began to swamp the boat, Jesus continued to rest peacefully. He looked, no doubt, so ordinary, so altogether human.

Yet when they reached desperation, the disciples cried out to Him, "Lord, save us!" Obviously, the disciples believed Jesus was the One who could deliver them. Probably they expected Him to call upon the Father for them, for they knew God would answer Him.

But Jesus stood up, and He spoke to the elements. Instantly "there was a great calm" (8:26; cf. Psalm 107:23–31). Of all Jesus' miracles, this was perhaps the most dramatic.

The disciples, too, were hushed. Then they whispered, "What kind of man is this?" Believing that Jesus was the Messiah, even the Son of God (John 1:41,49) did not prepare them for this reality: the man who had been exhausted, resting on a cushion, was the Creator and Ruler of the universe.

Discussing the Text

1. Why did Satan tempt Jesus to sin? Discribe your picture of what life today would be like if Jesus had sinned.

2. Why would the Spirit lead Jesus "into the desert to be tempted by the devil" (Matthew 4:1)?

3. List each of the temptations. Then next to each tell how Jesus resisted each.

4. How do the temptations Jesus encountered summarize the temptations all people face?

5. Why did the disciples cry out in desperation, "Lord, save us" (Matthew 8:25)? What did the disciples' cry indicate about their trust in themselves to deal with the storm? their trust in Jesus to deliver them from the storm?

6. Why did Jesus have to become a man?

Apply

A Christian writer has said, "Temptation provokes me to look upward to God." In obedience to His heavenly Father, Jesus answers temptation with the Word of God. Satan always seeks to raise doubts (the "ifs"), but Scripture responds firmly and clearly with the will and promises of God. Knowing the Bible is a precious asset through our struggles.

Through His Word, God offers us new courage, either for facing Satan's trials or in life crises. The devil must flee from God's people when they tell him to be gone (James 4:7), because Christ has asserted His power over Satan. Likewise, we can face dangers without fear, because Jesus is "in our boat." He may seem distant—sleeping on the cushion—but in fact He is always alert and powerful to command any dangers to cease.

Best of all, by withstanding the devil's temptations, Jesus was fully obedient to God in our place. Like Adam and Eve, we have all given in to the devil's whispers. But God sees Christ's perfect resistance to temptation and counts it as if it were our own. When we look back on yesterday's sins, we can picture ourselves forgiven and clothed in what Jesus has done. He is our life!

1. Do you agree or disagree with the statement, "Temptation provokes me to look upward to God"? Why or why not?

2. Read 2 Corinthians 12:9–10. When do we become strong in our battle against Satan?

3. How does God continue today to offer us power to resist the temptations of Satan? What does this say about seeking opportunities to worship and study God's Word?

4. "If you feel distant from God, guess who's moved?" How do people distance themselves from God? How does God remain constant even when people move?

5. Jesus climbed into our boats (lives) when we were baptized. How does this fact provide you comfort and hope as you face storms in life?

6. Jesus resisted the temptations of Satan, and on Calvary He won the victory over him. However, until the Day of Judgment, Satan will continue to deceive people on earth. What are some results of that deception in the world today?

7. How might we become involved in the battle against Satan and his deceptions?

Catechism Connection

Review the Seventh Petition of the Lord's Prayer and Luther's explanation in the opening for this session.

1. What assurance for your battles with Satan's temptations do you find in Psalm 121:7–8 and 2 Thessalonians 3:3?

2. Knowing God will deliver us from every evil, how may we view the hardships that we face? See Acts 14:22; Psalm 91:9–10; 2 Corinthians 12:9; and Hebrews 12:10–11.

3. Through faith in Christ, of what may we be certain, no matter what we face? See 2 Timothy 4:18.

Send

To Do This Week

Family Connection

1. Share with each other temptations you face. Agree to pray daily for each other that you might stand firm and resist these temptations.

2. Review the temptations of Jesus by the devil and the way that Jesus responded to each. Compare the temptations of Jesus to the temptations you face. How might Jesus' response to these temptations be helpful for you to remember?

3. Create cards to send to friends or loved ones who are experiencing temptations or storms in their lives. Write your favorite Bible passages on the cards to provide comfort to the one who will receive the card.

Personal Reflection

1. Reread the temptation account. Consider how at times Satan tempts you in the ways he tempted Jesus. Then read Jesus' response. Write Jesus' responses on the back of your business cards. Place the cards in your wallet. As you are tempted, pull out the cards and read Jesus' response.

2. Meditate on the stanzas of the hymn "How Precious Is the Book Divine" printed in the "Opening" activity.

For Next Week

Read John 4:1–42 in preparation for the next session.

Session 12

Jesus Accepts
a Samaritan Woman

(John 4:1–42)

Gather

Theme: No Sin Too Great!

Key Point

Jesus tells us that no sin is too great for Him to forgive. His death on the cross won for us forgiveness of all sins. His love enables us to share with others, "Your sins are forgiven."

Objectives

By the power of the Holy Spirit working through God's Word we will
1. summarize the significance of Jesus' words and actions to the Samaritan woman;
2. confess our sin and receive the comfort and assurance that no sin is too great for Jesus to forgive;
3. share with those burdened by sin the assurance of the forgiveness Jesus won for them on the cross.

Opening

Read responsively the following portion of Martin Luther's teachings about Baptism:

Leader: What benefits does Baptism give?

Group: It works forgiveness of sins, rescues from death and the devil, and gives eternal salvation to all who believe this, as the words and promises of God declare.

Leader: Which are these words and promises of God?

Group: Christ our Lord says in the last chapter of Mark: "Whoever believes and is baptized will be saved, but whoever does not believe will be condemned." [Mark 16:16]

Introduction

1. Although we may say that no sin is too great for God in Christ to forgive, how do our words and actions at times demonstrate a lack of confidence in this fact?

2. What is the danger for those who doubt the fact that no sin is too great for Jesus to forgive?

3. What is the danger for others we may know or have contact with if we doubt this fact?

4. How might we demonstrate this fact to others?

In today's lesson, we see Jesus reaching out to the despised and the forsaken with His forgiveness. Jesus' love is inclusive, for all people. We too are empowered by His love to share love with the despised and forsaken.

Study

Examine John 4:1–42.

Reading the Text

To be exclusive, to keep a good thing to oneself, is always a temptation. In today's lesson, Jesus reaches out to a woman many would have shunned. But He reaches out to her only with the pure truth of salvation—Himself.

The shortest route between the regions of Judea in the south and Galilee in the north went through the territory of Samaria. It would seem unremarkable, then, that Jesus and His disciples traveled that road (John 4:3–4). In fact, however, Jews would usually go well out of their way, crossing and then recrossing the Jordan to the east, rather than pass through Samaritan villages. The animosity between the two populations was very strong.

The Samaritans were a mixed people, descended from Israelites and the foreigners brought forcibly into the land by Assyrian conquerors seven centuries earlier (2 Kings 17:23–33). In the eyes of the Jews, not only was Samaritan blood impure, but their religion was corrupted; they had combined worship of Yahweh with the idolatries of the transplanted nations. The Samaritans accepted the Pentateuch, the first five books of the Old Testament, but rejected the rest. Their mutual hatred of the Jews was long and intense (Ezra 4:1–5, Luke 9:52–53).

The town of Sychar (John 4:5–6a) was symbolic of this rivalry. Near the larger ancient city of Shechem, it should have been a historic site for the Jews, for it was land purchased long ago by Jacob and given to his son Joseph (Genesis 33:18–19; 48:22). A well there, dug more than 100 feet deep through solid limestone by Jacob, is still used today. But it was near here that the kingdom of Israel had forever divided after the death of Solomon (1 Kings 12:1–19).

All of this explains the surprise a woman of the town felt when Jesus asked her for a drink (John 4:6–9). She easily recognized Jesus as a Jew—probably by the white fringe on His garment (rather than Samaritan blue) and certainly by His accent. The Jews ordinarily considered a man ceremonially unclean if his lips touched the drinking vessel of a Samaritan.

Moreover, as the conversation went on, the woman must have been even more intrigued by Jesus' interest in her. Jewish rabbis seldom spoke to women in public (hence the disciples' surprise, 4:27). A request for a drink was one thing, but Jesus considered her worthy also of serious theological discussion!

Most important, Jesus continued to care for the woman even though He knew her sordid past and present (4:16–18). Whether or not she was feeling burdened with guilt over her lifestyle, she doubtless knew the pain of exclusion. Women would not normally go to the well in the heat of day ("the sixth hour," or noon), so perhaps this woman was ostracized at the more "social" evening hour (cf. Genesis 24:11).

Just as Jesus is kind to speak to a sinful Samaritan woman at all, so He is gentle in His approach. Progressively He arouses her curiosity, moving from the secular (verses 7–9) to the spiritual (verses 10–12), offering her the greatest blessing (the "living water" in this case is eternal life, 4:13–15). He shows her need. She comes to know that He truly cares.

He cares for her, though, with the truth. He does not simply affirm her as she is. He moves the conversation steadily toward His intended teaching. That means He must confront her sin, and He must express a hard truth about God's plan of salvation: God has not chosen to work through her people (4:22). Salvation for the Samaritan will require accepting a Jewish Messiah; God's plan must always be accepted humbly, as it is. This alone is true worship (4:23–24).

Through the entire conversation, Jesus has one final destination in mind: Himself. Every new sentence is leading her nearer to Him. Finally the moment is right. She brings up the coming Messiah (4:25). "I who speak to you," Jesus says, "am He" (4:26). Jesus is the One who gives eternal life. Jesus is the One through whom the Father will be worshiped in truth. He is the One who cares enough to speak with an outcast Samaritan woman.

With such incredible news, she runs back to the village (4:28–29). "Could this be the Christ?" It seems too good to be true, but she believes it is. Soon, many others believe, too, first from her testimony and then from the words of Jesus Himself (4:39–42).

Jesus stays two days. It is an unscheduled stop, but this is why He has come—into the world and into Samaria (4:31–38). He understands that wherever He is, with whomever He is speaking, the time of harvest is now. Every moment and every soul is precious in God's purpose, because Jesus is the Savior of the whole world (4:42).

Discussing the Text

1. What historical events led to the animosity between Jews and Samaritans? See 2 Chronicles 36:20; Ezra 1:3–4; and Ezra 1–5.

2. Why would the woman have been intrigued by not only Jesus' request for water, but also the discussion He has with her?

3. Describe the progression of Jesus' conversation with the woman at the well? What kind of significance does this progression have for the woman? What is the final destination of His conversation?

4. How does the woman's response to the message Jesus has shared with her demonstrate the truth of Hebrews 4:12? How did others respond to that which the woman shared?

5. Describe the significance of the account of Jesus and the woman at the well for the Samaritans. For you. For all people.

Apply

Jesus' acts of kindness imply a double-sided application. On the one hand, and of first importance, we may identify ourselves as the recipients of Jesus' love, like the Samaritan woman. We may be certain that Jesus includes them in His salvation, because He has shown love regardless of gender, ethnic background, and moral history. To everyone, He reaches out personally, gently, pointing to Himself as Savior.

We can identify in the story with Jesus. That is, we are to be as inclusive of others as Jesus was with the woman at the well. There is no room in the church whatsoever for racism or any form of bigotry. Because Jesus died for all, we are called to be kind to all. Yet our kindness is to be expressed as Jesus expressed His—only in God's truth. It is not at all loving to compromise God's message just to be inclusive. Everyone needs to hear of his or her sin and of all the pure teachings of God's Word, whether they seem pleasant or not. To share with every soul all that we know to be true is genuine care and acceptance.

1. How are we like the Samaritan? How is God's message to the Samaritan woman a message to us also? See 1 Peter 2:24–25.

2. What comfort does the account of the Samaritan woman give to those who believe their sins are too great for Jesus to forgive? See, for example, Isaiah 1:18.

3. How might we reflect the acceptance that Jesus demonstrated to the woman at the well through our words and actions?

4. Some members of a congregation may have trouble accepting those who formerly had a wicked lifestyle, especially if cultural differences also exist. How do the actions of the early church in Acts 15:1–2, 19–21 suggest that we deal with the issue? What guidelines does Paul add in Ephesians 4:32?

Catechism Connection

Review Martin Luther's teaching about Baptism in the opening for this session.

1. Why is it appropriate to apply Jesus' words in John 3:5–7 to Baptism?

2. What does it mean to you that you have been baptized?

3. How can members of your congregation emphasize the importance of Baptism?

Send

To Do This Week

Family Connection

1. Review the story of the woman at the well. Ask, "How has Jesus treated us who are 'poor miserable sinners'?" Write thank-You notes to God.

2. The woman at the well eagerly told everyone of the love and forgiveness Jesus had provided to her. Have each family member identify people with whom they will share Jesus' love this week.

3. Read together Psalm 103.

Personal Reflection

1. Consider the magnitude of Jesus' love for you. Read Romans 5:6–11.

2. Share with someone who is experiencing guilt the "once for all" love and forgiveness of Jesus.

3. Consider how you might demonstrate Jesus' love for you by your words and actions. How might your acceptance of others provide you an opportunity to share Jesus' love for them?

For Next Week

Read John 9:1–41 in preparation for the next session.

Session 13

Jesus Gives Sight to a Man Born Blind

(John 9:1–41)

Gather

Theme: Who Sinned?

Key Point

In His greatest act of love, Jesus went to the cross to receive the punishment we deserved—death. His love for us motivates us to share His love with others so that they, too, may experience His forgiveness and confess Jesus as their Savior.

Objectives

By the power of the Holy Spirit working through God's Word, we will
1. share details of the account of the man born blind;
2. describe the reasons for the Pharisees' opposition to Jesus;
3. confess our sinful thoughts, words, and actions and receive the assurance of Jesus' forgiveness; and
4. share the love of Jesus with others.

Opening

Sing or speak together the first stanza of "Chief of Sinners Though I Be."

> Chief of sinners though I be,
> Jesus shed His blood for me,
> Died that I might live on high,
> Lives that I might never die.
> As the branch is to the vine,
> I am His, and He is mine.

Introduction

Many times people can be heard making statements such as these:
"Who broke the chair?"
"Who ate the last cookie?"
"Who made a mark on the wall?"
"Who sent the wrong bill to the customer?"

1. What "who" question have you recently heard or spoken?

2. When asked a "who" question, we can either respond "I did" or "I didn't." How must we all respond to the question "Who sinned?" Why?

In today's session the disciples ask the question "Who sinned?" in order to determine the cause of the blind man's affliction. Jesus teaches the disciples that the blindness was not a punishment for sin but an opportunity for Jesus to demonstrate God's saving work. Although all have sinned, Jesus came to earth to demonstrate God's saving work to all people through His death on the cross. By His death we receive life—on earth and into eternity.

Study

Examine John 9:1–41.

Reading the Text

In keeping with the movement of the church year, our sessions now progress steadily toward the climax of Jesus' ministry on earth. The story of Christ's passion, death, resurrection, and return to heaven begins with the rising opposition to His word and ministry.

Often the opposition to Christ arose over matters of Jewish worship tradition—interpretations and embellishments of Old Testament law that God had never intended. This is the case in the Pharisees' condemnation of Jesus for healing a blind man on the Sabbath. In fact, the conflict is between spiritual sight and spiritual blindness because Jesus' mission is to be the spiritual Light of the world.

Jesus and His disciples are in Jerusalem for one of the three annual festivals—the Feast of Booths or Tabernacles (John 7:2, 37; Leviticus 23:34–43). Jesus' preaching at the feast had very nearly caused some people to stone Him, for He had made some astounding claims: that all who believed in Him would receive the Holy Spirit (John 7:37–39), that He was the Light of the world (8:12), even that He was the eternal "I Am," existing long before Abraham (8:58–59; Exodus 3:13–14).

Now Jesus has occasion to illustrate what all of this means. Seeing a man who had been born blind, the disciples ask Jesus whose sin caused the man to suffer so (John 9:1–2). Rabbis of the day taught that afflictions were God's direct judgment for committing particular sins. When people were born with handicaps, others assumed the handicaps were a punishment either on the people who were handicapped or on their parents—for such sins as a wicked thought by the mother during pregnancy, or some sin committed by the person while still in the womb.

Jesus debunks that theory altogether (9:3–5). This man's blindness was no punishment, but rather an opportunity to show God's saving work. Again Jesus declares that He is the Light of the world, and this time He demonstrates it in a most tangible way (9:6–7). Still, Jesus intends more than just a physical healing. The Pool of

Siloam (see 2 Kings 20:20) to which Jesus sent the blind man was the source from which water was ceremonially drawn on the last day of the Feast of Tabernacles. Jesus had used this water in His illustration of the Holy Spirit (John 7:37–39). Jesus was therefore suggesting that very shortly the man would receive much more than his sight: he would receive the gift of faith that only the Spirit can give.

The Pharisees, though, are not at all pleased with Jesus' miracle. The fact that others "brought" the man to them (9:13) indicates that the Pharisees had already been very open about their hatred for Christ. Confronted with what they judged to be a blatant violation of the Sabbath (9:14–16), the Pharisees had to do something about Jesus or else lose face.

While God had, of course, forbidden work on the Sabbath (Exodus 20:8–10), the rabbis had pressed the commandment to extremes. For example, on the Sabbath, it was permissible to apply wine to one's eyelids, for that might be only for cleansing, but it was unlawful to apply it to the eye itself because then it might be for the purpose of healing. Worse though, saliva, which Jesus had used (John 9:6), could *never* be applied to the eyes on the Sabbath because it was always deemed to have healing value. Jesus exposed the folly of such distinctions. He would do God's work all the time, every day, because the time was short (5:16–17; 9:4).

Trying to discredit Jesus, the Pharisees conduct an inquiry into the former blind man and his parents (9:17–34). To confess Jesus as the Christ would carry dire consequences; to be "put out of the synagogue" (9:22) meant excommunication of the highest form. While certain offenses brought temporary suspension, this would be permanent. People who were "put out" were considered dead. No one was to eat or interact with them in any way—even to offer directions on the road. For this man and his parents, excommunication would mean utter desperation.

Yet the threats of the Pharisees only serve to bring forth a stronger confession of Jesus as the Son of God. Previously the man spoke of his benefactor as "the man they call Jesus" (9:11). Now he asserts, "He is a prophet" (9:17); and after further questioning, he declares that Jesus is "from God" (9:30–33).

This the Pharisees will not tolerate. With insults, they cast the man out of the synagogue (9:34). Ironically, they claim as their authority Moses (9:28–29), the very one whose writings Jesus says will condemn their unbelief (5:45).

Immediately Jesus comes looking for the man (9:35–38). "Do you believe in the Son of Man?" He asks. "Son of Man" was a well-recognized title for the Messiah (cf. Daniel 7:13–14; Matthew 26:63–64), which the man obviously understood. He wanted to believe in the Messiah, whoever He was, and he trusted Jesus to reveal Him. "You have now seen Him," Jesus says. "In fact, He is the one speaking with you." "Lord, I believe," the man gushes, falling down to worship Jesus.

The man's progression in confession is complete. Not only is Jesus a prophet, a man sent from God, but He is also the Savior. The man now had saving faith in Christ, given to him by the Holy Spirit. Jesus had opened the man's eyes not just to see the world, but to see Jesus as the Light of the world. This, more than the healing, was "the work of God" Jesus had promised would be displayed in the man's life (9:3). To reveal Himself as the Messiah was always a purpose of Jesus' caring miracles (Isaiah 35:5; 42:7).

Discussing the Text

1. How unusual do you think it would be today for someone to ask, "Who sinned?" (John 9:2) when they see a person who is blind or suffers some other affliction?

2. How did Jesus dispel the idea that a particular sin caused the man's blindness (9:3–5)?

3. Read verse 16. See also John 2:11. Describe the inner turmoil of the Pharisees. When might we face a similar turmoil?

4. Compare the responses of the man who received his sight (9:17b, 25, 27, 30–33) with that of his parents (9:20–21). How do you explain the difference?

5. How do verses 35–41 show Jesus' love for the man who had been blind?

6. What was the purpose of Jesus' miracles? What evidence do we have that Jesus fulfilled this purpose in the miracle?

Apply

This story is one of the most helpful in Scripture in explaining God's purpose for allowing affliction. Many people live with a fear that "God is going to get them" if they commit certain sins. They think thoughts like, "God made me fail in this job because I falsified that report last year," or "Mom got sick because I never told her about sneaking out to the fair." Certainly all suffering is a result of sin—the corruption that Adam and Eve brought into the world. And sin does sometimes have direct, painful consequences. (For example, using drugs can cause direct physical damage as well as emotional and spiritual problems.) But Scripture does not suggest that we look for a *specific* sin behind every affliction.

Rather, in the light of God's Word, every affliction can be seen as an opportunity for the work of God to be demonstrated. In this story, the man's blindness was not just an excuse for Jesus to prove He could do miracles. It was the first step in bringing the man to eternal joy, vitality, and health. Suffering is a reminder that we are frail and completely dependent on God. That understanding is a prerequisite for faith; people will not believe in a Savior unless they know they need one. This is what Jesus meant when He concluded the text, "If you were blind, you would not be guilty of sin; but now that you claim you can see, your guilt remains" (John 9:41). In other words, affliction is an effective preaching of the Law, a necessary preparation for the Gospel. God in His love may allow affliction so that we do not overlook His saving work.

Of course, showing us God's saving work is the purpose of the Light of the world. By this self-description, Jesus is telling us that in Him we see God and His love clearly. Life without Jesus is like walking in darkness, not knowing where we are going eternally, not understanding that God cares and forgives. When we see Jesus healing the blind, helping the poor, and dying for sins, we have a bright, vivid picture of God and of the future (John 12:45–46).

1. Compare sin and its natural consequences with the idea that God will punish people with affliction because of their sin.

2. How does every affliction provide God with an opportunity to demonstrate His work?

3. A boy lost his sight when he was 11 years old. He and his friends prayed that God would give him his sight back. When that didn't happen, they said that maybe some of his sin was stopping God's power from coming to him—maybe God was punishing him. What are some Bible verses you would want to share with this boy? Consider Romans 8:28–39 or Hebrews 12:2–3, 7–11.

4. How many blind people live in your community? Research shows that over 95 percent of blind people are not connected with a church. Therefore some churches are opening outreach centers where blind people can come once a week for support and for spiritual guidance. Could your congregation open such a center? For information and assistance, contact the Library for the Blind (toll-free) at 1-866-215-2455 or visit their Web site: www.blindmission.org.

5. Use the analogy of darkness and light to describe your relationship to God. Share your analogy with a partner.

6. How are we lights to the world?

Catechism Connection

Review the Second Article of the Apostles' Creed and Martin Luther's explanation in Sessions 2 and 3. Also read Isaiah 53.

1. The words of Isaiah 53:5 appear on the screen at the beginning of Mel Gibson's movie *The Passion of the Christ*. Why is this so appropriate?

2. Which other words from Isaiah 53 are especially meaningful to you?

3. When sharing portions of Isaiah 53 with someone, why might you also want to share John 3:16 or a similar verse?

Send

To Do This Week

Family Connection

1. Review the events in the story of the man born blind. Ask your family, "What did you learn from the story?"

2. Discuss the difference between darkness and light. Turn off all of the lights, so that the house is as dark as possible. Ask, "How does darkness make you feel?" Then light one candle and ask, "How does light, even the smallest of light, change your feelings?" Then remind your family members that God's Word often refers to people who live without Jesus as people living in darkness and to people who live with Jesus as people living in the light. Ask family members to describe what this analogy means to them.

3. Ask, "What is the 'chief' of something?" A chief is number one. "What does it mean when we sing 'Chief of sinners though I be, Jesus shed His blood for me'?"

Personal Reflection

1. Meditate on the words of the first stanza of "Chief of Sinners Though I Be." Consider the significance of the fact that Jesus willingly went to the cross to suffer and die for you—the chief of sinners.

2. Seek opportunities this week to tell someone about darkness and light. Help the person connect your discussion to Jesus who brought light into a world living in darkness because of sin.

For Next Week

Read Matthew 18:1–9 and 20:17–28 in preparation for the next session.

Adult Leader Guide

Session 1

John Prepares the Way for Jesus

(Luke 1:57–80; Matthew 3:1–12)

Gather

Theme: The Warmup to the Main Event!

Key Point and Objectives

Invite volunteers to read aloud the key point and objectives for this session.

Opening

Pray David's prayer from 1 Chronicles 29 together, followed by the Lord's Prayer.

Introduction

Read aloud the opening paragraph. Then discuss the questions that follow. If your group is large, you may want to assign participants to smaller groups so that all individuals have a chance to share.

1. Answers will vary. The lesser known performer will usually warm up the crowd.

2. If the warmup acts are of poor quality the crowd may become restless. Answers will vary.

Invite a volunteer to read aloud the closing paragraph.

Study

Read aloud or invite volunteers to read aloud Luke 1:57–80 and Matthew 3:1–12. Then invite volunteers to read aloud "Reading the Text." If time is limited, you may want to summarize the important points included in the commentary.

Discussing the Text

1. While most reactions may be similar, probably the neighbors and relatives of Elizabeth and Zechariah saw greater evidence of God's mercy, since they commonly viewed childlessness as a curse.

2. The name *John* was commanded by the angel Gabriel. The name means the "Lord is gracious."

3. In his song of praise Zechariah expresses his faith in God. The song describes future events as if they had already happened. John's coming and mission assured the fulfillment of God's plan for salvation.

4. John's ministry prepared the people for the coming of the Messiah. In this way, John was a warmup for the main event: God's promise of a Savior fulfilled in the person and work of Jesus Christ.

5. John commanded the people to repent of their sin. John also shared the Gospel as he proclaimed the coming of the kingdom of heaven with the arrival of the promised Messiah.

6. John's baptism gave the forgiveness of sins. In this way, John prepared people to receive the Messiah into their hearts.

Apply

Read aloud or invite volunteers to read aloud the opening paragraphs. Then discuss the questions that follow.

1. The Law shows people their sins and their need for a Savior. The Gospel shows people the forgiveness of sins and eternal life that Jesus won for all people on the cross. In a sense the Law is God's command to us—what we need to do. The Gospel is what God has done for us in Christ Jesus.

2. Through faith in Jesus we need not fear Judgment Day. Instead, in faith we look forward to the time when Jesus will come again and take us to live with Him forever in heaven.

3. In the Lord's Supper Jesus provides us His body and His blood. Through this body and blood God provides us forgiveness of sins. In heaven we will enjoy a never-ending feast of God's presence.

4. Answers will vary. Allow time for volunteers to share the meaning of their Baptisms with the entire group.

Catechism Connection

1. Jesus rules with all power, glory, and honor at the right hand of God.

2. Jesus guides our lives, motivating and empowering us to do the good works God prepared in advance for us to do.

3. We know we may bring every petition to Him, confident that He will answer our prayers according to His good and gracious will. Thus, we need not be anxious about anything; His peace fills our hearts.

Send

To Do This Week

Urge participants to do at least one of the suggested "Family Time" activities and one of the activities suggested in "Personal Reflection." Then close with prayer.

For Next Week

Urge participants to read the Scripture lessons appointed for the next session.

Session 2

An Angel Visits Mary

(Luke 1:26–55)

Gather

Theme: Highly Favored

Key Point and Objectives

Invite volunteers to read aloud the key point and objectives for this session.

Opening

Read the Second Article together. Then lead the group in prayer: Heavenly Father, we confess that because of sin, we deserve nothing other than eternal damnation. Thank You for love so great that You sent Your only Son to receive the punishment we deserve. Strengthen our faith, we pray, and finally give us the eternal life that Jesus earned for us. We pray in His name. Amen.

Introduction

Read aloud the opening paragraph. Then discuss the questions that follow.

1. A highly favored status (most favored nation status in the language of U.S. trade laws) allows a country to trade with another country with little red tape and greatly reduced import duties. It provides trade advantages.

2. A country must earn the trade status by demonstrating fairness in trade and economic benefit for both countries. Sometimes it must meet other criteria too.

3. Answers will vary. Because of sin we are unable to earn any status other than enemy of God. But God in His love for us sent Jesus to live a perfect life on our behalf and then receive the pun-

ishment we deserved because of our sin. Through Jesus' death on the cross we receive the forgiveness of sins and eternal life.

Read aloud the closing paragraph of this section. This paragraph is a bridge between the concepts developed in the introduction and the concepts that will be furthered explored in "Study."

Study

Read aloud Luke 1:26–55. Then invite volunteers to read aloud portions of "Reading the Text." If time is short you may wish to summarize the important facts included in the commentary.

Discussing the Text

1. The choice of a lowly virgin from humble surroundings is an early demonstration of God's grace; salvation comes through His great love, not through riches, fame, or human effort. Accept other reasonable answers.

2. At first, Mary was taken aback and puzzled by the angel's announcement of her "highly favored" status and her role as the mother of the Messiah. Finally, she yielded in humble obedience.

3. Mary and Joseph were both of the royal line of King David. God's hand is at work in this event. For no longer was David's line in power, nor did David's line hold the throne.

4. Jesus' name means "the Lord is salvation." The name marked Mary's son as the Savior of the world.

5. Mary asks, "How is this going to happen?" She simply puzzles over the immediate effect on herself and her future. She accepts the angel's message. Zechariah, on the other hand, asks for a sign.

6. Reread Mary's song of praise. Then invite volunteers to describe in their own words the message of the song. Answers will vary.

Apply

Read aloud or invite volunteers to read aloud the opening paragraphs of this section.

1. Through God all things are possible. God accepts us as we are—poor miserable sinners—and sent His only Son into this world to suffer and to die for our sins.

2. Through faith in Christ Jesus we are heirs of God's kingdom.

3. God's love for us and all people is immense. Invite participants to suggest other words that describe the enormity of God's love for all people revealed in the person and work of Jesus.

4. Participants may respond in various ways. Note that God keeps all His promises and that it isn't always necessary for Him to work through ordinary human means (method of conception, in this case), though He ordinarily does so.

Catechism Connection

1. In Matthew 1:25 God reveals that Joseph "had no union" with Mary until after Jesus was born. God assures us that God—not Joseph—is the father. Jesus *is* true God.

2. Only the sinless Son of God could save us. To do so it was necessary that He also be true man in order to act in our place under the Law and fulfill it for us. Thus, He had human attributes: He got hungry; He felt sorrow; He died; He slept; He could be touched; He wept; He thirsted; and so forth. (You will examine His divine attributes in the next session.)

Send

To Do This Week

Urge participants to complete one or more of the "Family Connection" activities and the "Personal Reflection" activities prior to the next time the study group meets. Then close with prayer.

For Next Week

Urge participants to read the assigned Scripture lessons prior to the next class session.

Session 3

Jesus Is Born

(Matthew 1:18–25; Isaiah 7:10–14)

Gather

Theme: God Intervenes!

Key Point and Objectives

Invite volunteers to read aloud the key point and objectives for this session.

Opening

Read Luther's explanation to the Second Article responsively. Then lead the group in prayer: Heavenly Father, once Your great love for us led You to intervene in the affairs of the world and send Your only Son to save us from the eternal death we deserved. Today we pray that you will open our hearts and minds to Your message of salvation and motivate us to share this Good News. We pray in Jesus' name. Amen.

Introduction

Say "intervention" loudly. Then read aloud the opening paragraph.

1. Answers will vary.

2. Answers will vary. Invite volunteers to share.

3. Answers will vary. People will usually intervene in the lives of people for whom they care and love.

Read aloud the closing paragraph. This paragraph provides a bridge between the concept developed in the introductory section and the concept that will be more fully developed as participants study Scripture.

Study

Read aloud Matthew 1:18–25 and Isaiah 7:10–14. Then invite volunteers to read aloud "Reading the Text." If time is short, you may wish to summarize the important facts included in the commentary.

Discussing the Text

1. The virgin birth is an essential doctrine of the Christian faith. God had revealed to Isaiah that the Savior would be born of a virgin, and God keeps His Word. The virgin birth positively identified Jesus, born of Mary, as the Promised One.

2. Answers will vary. Joseph must have experienced great disappointment when he learned Mary was pregnant, believing she had to have been unfaithful to him. Nevertheless, he cared for her and did not want to expose her to public disgrace or have her put to death. At the same time, he was unwilling to marry her.

3. Answers will vary. Probably Joseph was elated that he could marry the woman he loved without suspicion or disgrace. Certainly God led him to take this appropriate action. One could speculate on the sexual temptations Satan must have used during the months that followed.

4. *Immanuel* means "God with us." God is present with His people. The *el* in Immanuel teaches that the One true and powerful God is the God who is with us.

5. The virgin was with child, and the child is none other than Immanuel. We can be certain Jesus really is both true God and true man.

Apply

Read aloud or invite volunteers to read aloud the three paragraphs. Then discuss the questions that follow.

1. Jesus' name is useful in remembering the forgiveness He won for us through His death on the cross. His name means Savior.

2. God the Holy Spirit works through God's Word to create and to strengthen faith in Jesus. The Holy Spirit continues to work today to enable people to believe that which may seem impossible to believe.

3. Answers will vary.
4. Answers will vary.

Catechism Connection

1. Jesus had to be true man in order to act in our place under the Law and fulfill it for us and to be able to suffer and die in our place for our guilt. He had to be true God in order that His fulfilling of the Law, His life, suffering, and death might be a sufficient ransom for all people. Thus He was able to overcome death and the devil for us.

2. As true God, Jesus is almighty, omnipresent (present everywhere), eternal (without beginning or end), omniscient (all-knowing), and unchangeable.

3. Answers will vary.

Send

To Do This Week

Urge participants to complete one or more of the "Family Connection" activities and one or more of the "Personal Reflection" activities prior to the next time you meet. Then close with prayer.

For Next Week

Urge participants to read the assigned portion of Scripture prior to the next session.

Session 4

Wise Men Worship Jesus
(Matthew 2:1–12)

Gather

Theme: Inclusive: for Everyone

Key Point and Objectives

Invite volunteers to read aloud the key point and objectives for this session.

Opening

Speak together the words of Isaiah 42:6–7. Then lead the group in prayer: Thank You, Father, for Your boundless, inclusive love that led You to send Your only Son to win salvation for everyone. Move us, we pray, to respond to Your love and forgiveness by sharing Your love with all people. We pray in Jesus' name. Amen.

Introduction

1. Answers will vary. List all of the participants' ideas on a board or sheet of newsprint.

2. Answers will vary. Group the words that seem to go together.

3. Answers will vary.

4. Write a one- or two-sentence definition of inclusiveness using the labels created for each of the groups of words. Write the final definition for inclusiveness on the board.

Read aloud the closing paragraph.

Study

Read aloud Matthew 2:1–12. Then invite volunteers to read portions of "Reading the Text." If time is short, you may wish to summarize the important ideas shared in the commentary.

Discussing the Text

1. God's actions stand out in this account. He inspired the messages of Balaam and Jeremiah, He led Jewish settlers to share the words of Scripture, and He moved the Wise Men to follow the star. God—His plan of salvation—is the main actor of the story.

2. Magi were members of a caste of wise men who studied the heavenly bodies as well as medicine and other natural sciences. The Magi were not kings.

3. Herod was suspicious of anyone with a legitimate claim to the throne. He was threatened by the king of whom the Magi spoke.

4. The gifts expressed the Magi's faith and joy of salvation. The gifts may have symbolized the person and work of Jesus; gold befitting a king, frankincense burned in worship, and myrrh a sweet-smelling gum used to prepare bodies for burial. Very likely God led the Wise Men to bring gifts with more meaning than they understood.

5. God warned the Wise Men to avoid Herod on their return home.

6. God clearly taught in the account of the Wise Men that Jesus had come to save all people—both Jews and Gentiles.

7. God wants everyone to be saved. For it was God who was working in history. God caused a pagan prophet to speak a promise about the coming Savior (Numbers 22:16–19; 24:17). God invited the Wise Men to visit the Christ. God protected the Wise Men and the child from Herod. God announced that salvation was for all people. The Wise Men were recipients of God's grace.

Apply

Read aloud or invite volunteers to read aloud the two paragraphs. Then discuss the questions that follow.

1. Each of us no matter who we are, no matter what we have done, belong to Christ's kingdom by God's grace through faith. Jesus came to win salvation for all people—Jews and Gentiles.

2. God's message to us through the Wise Men is that God invites all people to receive the forgiveness of sins and eternal life through the person and work of Jesus. We then witness the birth of Jesus as guests of honor, not just passersby.

3. Motivated by God's love for us, the chief of sinners, we joyfully seek opportunities to share His love with others.

4. Answers will vary.

Catechism Connection

1. As our Prophet Jesus brings us the Gospel—the words of eternal life.

2. Jesus gave Himself as a sacrifice for our sin and still pleads for us with His heavenly Father. He also fulfilled the Law perfectly in our stead (Galatians 4:4–5).

3. Jesus' kingdom is a spiritual kingdom, one He built as He lived and died for us. Finally He will rule in His heavenly kingdom (2 Timothy 4:18).

Send

To Do This Week

Urge participants to complete one or more of the "Family Connection" activities and one or more of the "Personal Reflection" activities prior to the next time the class meets. Then close with prayer.

For Next Week

Urge participants to read the assigned Scripture lesson in preparation for the next session.

Session 5

Mary and Joseph Take Jesus to Egypt

(Matthew 2:13–23)

Gather

Theme: God's Itinerary

Key Point and Objectives

Invite volunteers to read aloud the key point and objectives for this session.

Opening

Read the First Article and Luther's explanation responsively. Then lead the group in prayer: Loving Father, Your divine power led Mary and Joseph to take whatever action was necessary for You to accomplish the work of salvation through Your Son. We pray, give us the faith to trust You to guide our lives and help us to know that nothing can separate us from the love You give us in Christ Jesus, our Savior. We pray in His name. Amen.

Introduction

1. Answers will vary. Invite volunteers to share their responses.
2. Answers will vary. Our own agendas, our sin, or the sins of others might challenge God's itinerary for our lives.
3. Answers will vary.

Read aloud the closing paragraph.

Study

Read aloud Matthew 2:13–23. Then invite volunteers to read aloud portions of "Reading the Text." If time is short, you may wish to summarize for the class the important facts shared in the commentary.

Discussing the Text

1. God was in complete control of the events in this account. He would not let any human being keep Him from accomplishing His plan of salvation.

2. Hosea 11:1 indicates clearly that God intended to bring His Son out of Egypt. Matthew understands and affirms that Jesus is the fulfillment of the entire Old Testament.

3. The words of Jeremiah signaled the fulfillment in Christ's coming—the sorrow of the mothers for their children. It clearly reveals that all God has promised in the Old Testament was being fulfilled and would be fulfilled in the person and work of Jesus.

4. Already when God inspired the Old Testament, He knew the evil that Herod would carry out. (He did not cause it!) God, then, worked through some of Herod's evil actions to fulfill prophecy. No evil could prevent God from carrying out His plan of salvation.

Apply

Read aloud or invite volunteers to read aloud the opening paragraphs. Then discuss the questions that follow.

1. Answers will vary.

2. Satan, the world, and our own sinful self have no control over us. Satan was defeated through Jesus' death. Through His death and resurrection, Jesus provides us assurance of our own resurrection from the dead. Death has no power over us.

3. Answers will vary.

4. Answers will vary. Invite volunteers to share specific ways in which they might more effectively share with others God's itinerary for them.

5. Answers will vary. Perhaps we would share some of God's assurances in Romans 8:18–39. If God loves us so much that He would sacrifice His only Son for us (verse 32), most certainly He will not stop loving us now!

Catechism Connection

1. God keeps His promise to care for us. He is working for our good even when we may think He has deserted us.

2. Instead of worrying, Jesus instructs us to seek God's kingdom and His righteousness.

Send

To Do This Week

Urge participants to complete one or more of the "Family Connection" activities and one or more of the "Personal Reflection" activities prior to the next time the class meets. Then close with prayer.

For Next Week

Urge participants to read the assigned portion of Scripture prior to the next class session.

Session 6

John Baptizes Jesus

(Matthew 3:13–17)

Gather

Theme: A Representative

Key Point and Objectives

Invite volunteers to read aloud the key point and objectives for this session.

Opening

Read Luther's explanation of the blessings of Baptism together. Then lead the group in prayer: Merciful God, we thank You for granting us new birth in Holy Baptism, making us heirs of Your heavenly kingdom. We pray, keep us in our baptismal grace that according to Your good pleasure we may faithfully lead a godly life and finally obtain the promised inheritance in heaven; through Jesus Christ, our Lord. Amen.

Introduction

Read aloud the introductory facts. Then discuss the questions that follow.

1. A representative represents his/her constituency.

2. A representative must be perceived by his/her constituency as truly representing them and their needs and concerns.

Read aloud the closing paragraph of this section.

Study

Read aloud Matthew 3:13–17. Then invite volunteers to read aloud portions of "Reading the Text." If time is short, you may wish to summarize the main facts shared in the commentary.

Discussing the Text

1. Jesus desired to be baptized to fulfill all that was required of sinful human beings. John at first did not understand why he should baptize Jesus because his baptism was for the forgiveness of sins, and Jesus was without sin.

2. Jesus' baptism accompanied by the voice and appearance of God the Father and God the Holy Spirit was God's public seal of approval of Jesus as the Messiah. His sacrifice for our sin is sufficient for all times.

3. The anointing of the Holy Spirit prepared Jesus for the temptation that would occur in the desert.

4. Though He had no sin, Jesus became sin so that we could receive His righteousness. By His death He freed us from slavery to Satan.

5. Jesus is identified by the voice of God the Father as the Son of God. The Holy Spirit descended upon Jesus in the form of a dove.

Apply

Read aloud or invite volunteers to read aloud the opening paragraphs. Then discuss the questions that follow.

1. Jesus placed Himself in unity with all sinful people by being baptized. He stands before God clothed in our sin. He is ready to accomplish the purpose for which God sent Him to earth; and, ultimately, to earn for sinful people forgiveness of sins and eternal life through His death on the cross.

2. The Father declares His pleasure that Jesus willingly assumed the guilt of our sin. Because Jesus perfectly carried out God's plan for our salvation, we have forgiveness of sins and eternal life. There is no salvation in any other.

3. Answers will vary. Provide time for volunteers to share.

4. Answers will vary. God has given status to each of His children. We are *God's* sons and daughters!

5. Without the Holy Spirit we would fail to carry out the tasks God has given us.

6. Answers will vary. While we may approach some tasks with humility or fear, we can always be sure the Spirit is ready to give whatever wisdom and strength we need.

Catechism Connection

1. Through Baptism, we receive the blessings Christ has earned for us. (Baptism is a means of grace.)

2. The jailer received faith—the one essential element of salvation—through Paul's preaching. Immediately he desired Baptism, in accordance with God's command. To refuse Baptism would be to reject the grace God gives us in the Sacrament.

Send

To Do This Week

Urge participants to complete one or more of the "Family Connection" activities and one or more of the "Personal Reflection" activities prior to the next time the class meets. Then close with prayer.

For Next Week

Urge participants to read the assigned portions of Scripture in preparation for the next class session.

Session 7

Jesus Calls Us to Follow Him

(John 1:29–41; Matthew 9:9–13)

Gather

Theme: Hospital or Museum

Key Point and Objectives

Invite volunteers to read aloud the key point and objectives for this session.

Opening

Read Luther's explanation of Baptism. Then lead the group in prayer: Heavenly Father, the great love You have shown to us through Your Son Jesus moves us to repent of our sin. We pray that You will also motivate and empower us to demonstrate Your love, living each day as Your disciples. Hear us for Jesus' sake. Amen.

Introduction

Read aloud the quote. Then discuss the questions that follow.
1. Answers will vary.
2. The church is a place for sinners, where God declares His free grace to all people through the person and work of Jesus. When a church becomes a place for its members to show off their good works, it loses the focus which Jesus intended for His church.
3. Answers will vary.

Study

Read aloud or invite volunteers to read aloud John 1:29–41 and Matthew 9:9–13. Then, if time permits, invite volunteers to read aloud "Reading the Text." If time is short, you may wish to summarize the important facts included in the commentary.

Discussing the Text

1. Jesus always chooses His disciples. There is nothing we can do to earn Jesus' favor. Jesus calls us through His Word to faith.

2. John's announcement would have been exciting to the Jewish ear. The Lamb of God was a symbol for the promised Messiah.

3. Andrew shared his excitement with his brother Simon. Peter would come to be a "rock," strong in faith. John is the author of the gospel by his name. James was the brother of John. Matthew was a tax collector for the Roman government.

4. We would never have chosen Matthew to be one of the disciples, because he was a tax collector for the Roman government, and therefore despised by his own people. To the people of his day, particularly the religious leaders, Matthew was considered the "lowest of the low."

5. Rabbis considered repentance something that people had to do to make themselves acceptable to God. Jesus makes it clear that His act of love brings about true repentance.

Apply

Invite volunteers to read aloud the opening paragraphs. Then discuss the questions that follow.

1. Since Jesus calls us to be His disciples, we can't refuse. We never need to doubt that we are Jesus' disciples since He chose us and claimed us through Baptism as His own. He justifies us and makes us heirs of His glory.

2. Through Baptism we were marked for lifelong commitment to Jesus.

3. Jesus' love and forgiveness for us motivates and empowers us to demonstrate His love and forgiveness to others.

4. Answers will vary. Remind participants that in discipleship God is active. We respond to God, because of what He first did for us.

5. Answers will vary. Be sure to discuss the power needed for any changes in behavior—power God provides through His Word, Baptism, and the Lord's Supper.

Catechism Connection

1. The water of the Great Flood destroyed the evil that surrounded Noah in his day; the water of Baptism destroys the evil power of Satan to control us. Thus, both Noah and we are saved by water.

2. On the cross Christ suffered the punishment for our sins, winning the victory over Satan. His death would have no value without His resurrection from the dead.

3. Through Baptism the Holy Spirit empowers us to do God's will in our lives, resulting in a good conscience. Also, we can be sure all our sins are forgiven.

Send

To Do This Week

Urge participants to complete one or more of the "Family Connection" activities and one or more of the "Personal Reflection" activities prior to the next class session. Then close with prayer.

For Next Week

Urge participants to read the assigned portions of Scripture in preparation for the next class session.

Session 8

Jesus Helps Us Love
and Forgive One Another

(Matthew 18:21–35; Mark 10:13–16; 1 Corinthians 1:10–17)

Gather

Theme: How Many Times?

Key Point and Objectives

Invite volunteers to read aloud the key point and objectives for this session.

Opening

Read the Fifth Petition of the Lord's Prayer and Luther's explanation responsively. Then lead the group in prayer: Father, You know how unloving we can be at times. Yet You continue to forgive us. Help us to appreciate Your great love for us and thus to be willing to forgive everyone who sins against us, no matter what that person has done. Grant this for the sake of Jesus, our Savior. Amen.

Introduction

Ask, "How many times must I forgive someone who continually sins against me?" Then discuss the questions that follow.

1. Answers will vary. The magnitude of the forgiveness they have received often provides a clue to the amount of forgiveness people are willing to provide.

2. Answers will vary. Invite volunteers to share, but don't force anyone to share.

3. God answers the question, "As many times as they sin against you." His love and mercy for sinners, who continually sin against Him, is endless. His mercy endures forever.

Read aloud the closing paragraph.

Study

Read aloud or invite volunteers to read aloud portions of Matthew 18:21–25; Mark 10:13–16; and 1 Corinthians 1:10–17. If time permits, read aloud "Reading the Text" for additional insights.

Discussing the Text

1. By rabbinic practice, a repeat sinner was to be forgiven no more than three times. By Peter sharing a more generous portion of forgiveness, seven times, he tests whether or not he understands the essence of Jesus' parable. Obviously, Peter does not fully grasp the magnitude of God's forgiveness and God's desire for His forgiven children to forgive others.

2. Jesus' response indicates that forgiveness can never be numbered. Forgiving others is limitless because Jesus never stops forgiving us.

3. We, like the servant, could never repay our debt to God. But God paid our debt in full through His only Son's death on the cross.

4. God expects us to treat a brother or sister with the same forgiveness and love that He has demonstrated to us through Christ.

5. Jesus offers His love and mercy to all, including the children. Spending time with children was beneath the dignity of a rabbi, but Jesus welcomes the children, takes them in His arms, and blesses them.

6. Factions arose in the Corinthian church. Paul pointed the people to Christ and His cross.

Apply

Read aloud or invite a volunteer to read aloud the opening paragraphs. Then discuss the questions that follow.

1. Answers will vary. Provide time for volunteers to share their responses to this question.

2. Because I am certain that Jesus has forgiven me, the "chief" sinner, then I am eager to show the same love and forgiveness to others.

3. Jesus desires that we accept all people. He desires that we share His love and mercy with all people.

4. Have participants take a few moments to write a prayer giving thanks to God for the forgiveness Jesus won for us on the cross. Include also in the prayer a petition requesting that you would be motivated by Jesus' love to love and to forgive others.

5. "That's okay" could suggest overlooking sin, whereas "I forgive you" demonstrates a willingness to follow the instructions of Jesus.

6. Too often we are tempted to rely upon our own strength to overcome a difficult situation. Peter reminds us to turn instead to the strength God provides. We receive this through God's Word, Baptism, and the Lord's Supper.

Catechism Connection

1. After giving the Lord's Prayer to His disciples, Jesus repeats the importance of forgiveness in the life of a Christian.

2. Answers will vary. We might want to read these verses when we are overwhelmed with our sin.

3. God's mercy moves us to be kind, compassionate, and forgiving to one another.

Send

To Do This Week

Urge participants to complete one of more of the "Family Connection" activities and one or more of the "Personal Reflection" activities during the coming week. Then close with prayer.

For Next Week

Urge participants to read the assigned portions of Scripture in preparation for the next session.

Session 9

Jesus Teaches His
Disciples to Trust Him

(Matthew 5:1–12; 14:22–33)

Gather

Theme: "Trust Me"

Key Point and Objectives

Invite volunteers to read aloud the key point and objectives for this session.

Opening

Read the First Commandment and Luther's explanation responsively. Then lead the group in prayer: Thank You, heavenly Father, for leading us to recognize our sin, for rescuing us from that sin, and for the many other blessings You give us. Move us, we pray, to trust You completely in every situation we face. Hear us for Jesus' sake. Amen.

Introduction

Say loudly, "Trust me!" Then discuss the questions that follow.
1. Answers will vary.
2. Answers will vary. Most of us have learned through unpleasant experiences that even if someone tells us that we can trust him/her, we have no assurance that he/she will demonstrate trustworthiness.
Read aloud the closing paragraph of this section.

Study

Read aloud or invite volunteers to read aloud Matthew 5:1–12 and 14:22–33. Then invite volunteers to read aloud portions of "Reading the Text." If time is short, you may wish to summarize the important facts included in the commentary.

Discussing the Text

1. Jesus assures believers that they are blessed, even when circumstances seem to indicate otherwise.

2. Answers will vary. Encourage discussion.

3. The Beatitudes are not a "how to" manual for happiness. Instead, they are a description of what Christians already are and of the blessings that Christians already possess through faith in Christ Jesus.

4. Each of the Beatitudes begins with a form of the Greek word *makarios*. This describes a blessed condition rather than a blessing given. Jesus points to the fact that those who possess saving faith in Him are already blessed.

5. The sea was known for its sudden and deadly storms. It is not surprising that the disciples are frightened by the storm.

6. Although Jesus reproves Peter for his "little faith," He does acknowledge the fact that Peter does have faith.

7. When we confess our sins we plead, "Lord, save me," acknowledging that on our own we are helpless to save ourselves.

8. The disciples respond in amazement and then confess their faith in the words, "Truly, You are the Son of God!" We respond to the forgiveness of sins and eternal life that Jesus won for us on the cross in amazement of His grace and mercy, and by confessing Him as our Lord and Savior.

Apply

Read aloud or invite volunteers to read aloud the opening paragraphs. Then discuss the questions that follow.

1. Jesus is always present to bless and to protect us. Jesus is "God with us."

2. Our actions are insignificant in comparison to God's action on our behalf. We can do nothing to earn God's favor and His love.

We can do nothing to stop the storms that may occur in our lives. But in Christ we have the assurance of God's love and favor in spite of our sins. Jesus travels with us through the storms that may blow up in our lives.

3. Jesus continues to forgive us for our sin. He constantly saves us from the deadly results of our lack of trust. We can be confident that nothing can separate us from the love of God in Christ Jesus.

4. Spoken sincerely, the reply suggests gratefulness for the blessings we receive from God. We could expect great differences in the way others respond to those words.

5. The Beatitudes point us to rich blessings God has given us. Faith in the God who has given those blessings leads to "godliness with contentment."

Catechism Connection

1. God requires perfect love to Himself and to others.

2. We are not able to follow God's law of love. Therefore He sent Jesus to take the punishment. Through faith we receive His righteousness; we have been reconciled with God. Now we desire to live according to His law of love.

3. Even the devil *knows* God's law of love. Faith also acknowledges our unworthiness and trusts God for forgiveness through the blood of Jesus.

Send

To Do This Week

Urge participants to complete one or more of the "Family Connection" activities and one or more of the "Personal Reflection" activities prior to the next class session. Then close with prayer.

For Next Week

Urge participants to read the appointed Scripture lessons in preparation for the next class session.

Session 10

Jesus Shows His Glory

(Matthew 17:1–9)

Gather

Theme: Ah Hah!

Key Point and Objectives

Invite volunteers to read aloud the key point and objectives for this session.

Opening

Sing or read the stanzas from "How Good, Lord, to Be Here." Then lead the group in the following prayer, adapted from *The Lutheran Hymnal*: O God, who in the glorious transfiguration of Your only-begotten Son confirmed the mysteries of the faith by the testimony of the fathers, and who, in the voice that came from the bright cloud, did in a wonderful manner foreshadow the adoption of sons, mercifully keep Your promise to make us coheirs with the King of His glory and bring us to the enjoyment of the same; through Jesus Christ, Your Son, our Lord. Amen.

Introduction

Once again say, "Ah Hah!" Then discuss the questions that follow.

1. Answers will vary.

2. Answers will vary. Allow time for volunteers to share their faith as they respond to this question.

Read aloud the closing paragraph of this section.

Study

Read aloud or invite volunteers to read aloud portions of Matthew 17:1–9. Then read aloud "Reading the Text." If time is short, you may wish to summarize the important points.

Discussing the Text

1. The Transfiguration is the revealing to, or "shining upon," the nations. It strengthens the disciples for the faith-shaking events that would soon come. The Transfiguration for us shows Jesus' glory in our midst.

2. Scripture does not reveal why Jesus chose these three disciples to witness this event. Certainly He was preparing them for the events that would follow His death, resurrection, and ascension—some of which would lead to death (Acts 12:2).

3. Answers may vary. Probably Jesus' brightness would remind the disciples of God's glory (Exodus 40:34–38). Talk about the importance of this as they went about the post-Good Friday activities.

4. Likely Peter, James, and John had been told about the Father's message at Jesus' Baptism. These words must have been very reassuring during some of the dark days that followed.

5. Moses and Elijah represent the entire Old Testament. They represent the Old Testament Scriptures often referred to as "the Law and the Prophets." Jesus would soon accomplish all that was promised in the Old Testament.

6. Peter failed to understand the necessity for Jesus to suffer. He didn't grasp the uniqueness of Jesus and His mission.

7. The disciples understood who Jesus was, but they didn't fully comprehend the work that Jesus still needed to complete. Not until after the Resurrection would the significance of the Transfiguration make complete sense to them.

Apply

Read aloud or invite volunteers to read aloud the opening paragraphs. Then discuss the questions that follow.

1. Jesus remains our encouragement, our hope, and our confidence in any and all situations we may face. He is truly the Son of God, who possesses all authority and power.

2. The disciples saw Jesus in His glory—face to face! That is the joy of heaven. No wonder they didn't want to leave. When we enter heaven, we will see Him as He is—and will never have to leave.

3. Whatever we face in this life, we have the complete assurance that we will live forever in the radiance of Christ. We can always look forward to that which Jesus has prepared for us—a place in heaven.

4. Paul had seen wonderful visions but learned that he had to depend on God's grace. Without that grace we would never receive the glory that awaits us in heaven.

Catechism Connection

1. He descended into hell. The third day He rose again from the dead. He ascended into heaven and sits at the right hand of God, the Father Almighty. From thence He will come to judge the living and the dead.

2. God exalted Christ that all would confess Him as Lord.

3. Christ is interceding for us.

Send

To Do This Week

Urge participants to complete one or more of the suggested "Family Connection" activities and one or more of the "Personal Reflection" activities prior to the next time the class meets. Then close with prayer.

For Next Week

Urge participants to read the assigned Scripture lesson in preparation for the next class session.

Session 11

Jesus Shows His Power

(Matthew 4:1–11; 8:23–27)

Gather

Theme: Power!

Key Point and Objectives

Invite volunteers to read aloud the key point and objectives for this session.

Opening

Read the Seventh Petition and Luther's explanation responsively. Then lead the group in prayer: Heavenly Father, on our own we do not have the power to resist the temptations of Satan. Thank You for sending Your Son to defeat Satan and thereby giving us the power to resist his temptations. Move us, we pray, to seek opportunities to strengthen our faith through the power of the Holy Spirit working through Your Word. In Jesus' name we pray. Amen.

Introduction

1. Answers will vary.
2. Answers will vary.
3. Answers will vary.

Read aloud the paragraph that summarizes the discussion on power and guides participants into the scriptural study for the day.

Study

Read aloud or invite volunteers to read aloud portions of Matthew 4:1–11 and 8:23–27. Then invite volunteers to read aloud portions of "Reading the Text." If time is short, you may wish to summarize the important facts.

Discussing the Text

1. If Satan could cause Jesus to commit just one sin, every soul would be lost to hell. There would be no one who could fulfill perfectly the demands of the Law. Talk about how the world might be different if Jesus had sinned

2. To win a victory over an enemy, there must be a confrontation. God does not reveal why He chose this time and place.

3. First, the devil tempted Jesus to doubt His heavenly Father's ability to provide; "Tell these stones to become bread." Jesus responds to the temptations with the words of Deuteronomy 8:3. In the second temptation, the devil suggests an easy way for Jesus to fulfill His destiny. Jesus responds by speaking God's Word found in Deuteronomy 6:16. In the third temptation, the devil offers Jesus all the kingdoms of the world if He only worships him. Jesus responds with the words of Deuteronomy 6:13.

4. The temptations of Jesus epitomize the temptations we experience: the desire for material things, for popularity, for power.

5. The disciples believed Jesus was the One who could deliver them. The disciples realized they were powerless to deal with the storm. They trusted Jesus to deliver them.

6. By becoming a man, Jesus became subject to the Law and to temptation, as Adam was. The first Adam had fallen to Satan's temptation and brought God's judgment on himself and on nature. The second Adam fulfilled God's Law perfectly, resisting all temptation, and brought redemption from sin and judgment. We, and nature, have this now, but still await full revelation of this when He comes again.

Apply

Read aloud or invite a volunteer to read aloud the opening paragraphs of this section. Then discuss the questions that follow.

1. Answers will vary. We realize as Christians that we are unable to withstand temptations on our own. Instead we depend upon the power that enabled Jesus to withstand temptations to empower us to turn away from temptation.

2. We become strong when we realize our own weakness and, therefore, rely upon God's grace for strength.

3. Through His Word and Sacrament, God continues to

empower us. The Holy Spirit works through Word and Sacrament to strengthen our faith, enabling us to withstand the devil's temptations. We need to continue to seek opportunities to hear and to study God's Word.

4. God never distances Himself from people. Instead, as people move away from opportunities to study God's Word, they are also removing themselves from the faith-strengthening power God desires to provide. God's Word is unchanging.

5. Answers will vary. Provide time for volunteers to share.

6. Satan will be completely chained on Judgment Day. Invite participants to share ways they have seen him attempt to bring people into his evil kingdom.

7. Certainly people need to be made aware of Satan's deceptions. Answers will vary.

Catechism Connection

1. We know we can count on God to be with us. He gives us the power to resist Satan's temptations.

2. Answers may vary. Our weaknesses and the hardships we face often become opportunities for us to see God's power or the need to rely upon His grace. God always works for our good; He seeks to lead us to eternal life.

3. We know God *will* rescue us and bring us safely to His heavenly kingdom.

Send

To Do This Week

Urge participants to complete one or more of the "Family Connection" activities and one or more of the "Personal Reflection" activities prior to the next time the class meets. Then close with prayer.

For Next Week

Urge participants to read the assigned Scripture lesson in preparation for the next class session.

Session 12

Jesus Accepts
a Samaritan Woman

(John 4:1–42)

— Gather —

Theme: No Sin Too Great!

Key Point and Objectives

Invite volunteers to read aloud the key point and objectives for this session.

Opening

Read responsively the printed section of Luther's explanation of Baptism. Then lead the group in prayer: We confess, heavenly Father, that we sin against You daily and often. Sometimes our sins may seem ready to overwhelm us. Continue to forgive us, dear God, and send Your Spirit to assure us that, since Jesus already suffered the punishment for our sins, they need not burden us. In His name we pray. Amen.

Introduction

1. Answers will vary. At times our guilt can overwhelm us, even though we know and affirm that Jesus died on the cross to win for us complete forgiveness for all sins. Jesus has forgiven us. We may have difficulty forgiving ourselves. Satan would have us believe that our sins are too great for Jesus to forgive.

2. They may experience guilt or believe that Jesus will not forgive their sins.

3. Doubting this fact leads people ultimately to despair. They doubt the forgiveness Jesus won for them on the cross. Ultimately, they doubt their salvation.

4. By sharing the hope that lives within us, we witness the assurance of the complete forgiveness of sins and eternal life that Jesus has won for all people.

Read aloud or invite a volunteer to read aloud the closing paragraph.

Study

Read aloud or invite volunteers to read aloud portions of John 4:1–42. Then read aloud "Reading the Text." If time is short, you may wish to summarize the important facts included in this commentary.

Discussing the Text

1. At the time of Nebuchadnezzar the Jews were taken into exile and others were brought in to work the land. When Cyrus allowed exiles to return, those living there (ancestors of the Samaritans) resented those who returned.

2. The woman was probably intrigued because Jesus asked for water from a Samaritan, and Jews generally considered a man ceremonially unclean if his lips touched the drinking vessel of a Samaritan. Also, Jesus considered her worthy enough to demonstrate care for her and enter into a theological discussion with her.

3. Jesus moves from the secular to the spiritual. He shows the woman her need. He demonstrates care for her. He confronts her sin. He expresses truth about God's plan for salvation. Ultimately, the final destination of the conversation is Jesus, who alone can provide the woman that which she most desperately needs—forgiveness of sins and eternal life.

4. Jesus' words were powerful and active. The woman ran back to the village and told others of Him. Soon many people believed from her testimony and then from the words of Jesus Himself.

5. Jesus offers forgiveness of sins and eternal life to all sinners. Answers will vary.

Apply

Read aloud or invite volunteers to read aloud the opening paragraphs of this section. Then discuss the questions that follow.

1. We are sinners like the Samaritans, unworthy of Jesus' love and forgiveness. Jesus provides to us the same forgiveness of sins and eternal life He gave to the woman at the well.

2. No sin is too great for Jesus to forgive. He eagerly and willingly forgives all sins.

3. As we accept others, we are able to demonstrate the love Jesus demonstrated to the woman at the well.

4. First of all, problems need to be discussed openly, asking God for guidance. At times we may need to adjust traditions so that people who are "different" feel they are being welcomed. In all things, God's compassion must abound.

Catechism Connection

1. It is the Spirit who works through the water and Word of Baptism to create and sustain faith.

2. Answers will vary. We can be sure that we are God's children, members of His family, forgiven, strengthened, and so forth.

3. Answers will vary.

Send

To Do This Week

Urge participants to complete one or more of the suggested "Family Connection" activities and one or more of the suggested "Personal Reflection" activities prior to the next time the class meets. Then close with prayer.

For Next Week

Urge participants to read the assigned portion of Scripture in preparation for the next class session.

Session 13

Jesus Gives Sight to a Man Born Blind

(John 9:1–41)

Gather

Theme: Who Sinned?

Key Point and Objectives

Invite volunteers to read aloud the key point and objectives for this session.

Opening

Sing or speak together the first stanza of "Chief of Sinners Though I Be." Then lead the group in prayer: Thank You, dear Savior, for the great sacrifice You made for us. Now, assured of the forgiveness You earned, may Your Spirit empower us to tell others of Your great love. In Your name we pray. Amen.

Introduction

Invite a volunteer to read aloud with expression each of the statements. Then discuss the questions that follow. If your study group is large, you may want to assign participants to smaller groups so that everyone has a chance to share.

1. Answers will vary. "Who" questions usually seek the perpetrator of a crime.

2. We must all respond to the question "Who sinned?" with "I did." Scripture teaches that all have sinned: "Sin entered the world through one man, and death through sin, and in this way death came to all men, because all sinned" (Romans 5:12).

Read aloud the closing paragraph of the "Introduction." This paragraph serves as a bridge to the concepts that will be taught in the session.

Study

Read aloud John 9:1–41 and the commentary included in the "Reading the Text" section. You may wish to ask volunteers to read portions of both.

Discussing the Text

Discuss the Scripture lesson using the questions in this section. Once again, if your class is large, you may want to divide it into small groups so that all of the participants have a chance to share.

1. Some in your group may know individuals who have made the same conclusion as that taught by the Jewish leaders—that afflictions are a direct judgment for particular sins.

2. Jesus tells His disciples that the man's blindness is not a punishment for a particular sin, but instead an opportunity to demonstrate God's saving work. In declaring that He is the Light of the world and by performing the miracle, Jesus teaches that He is not only the One sent by God to heal the afflicted from physical ailments but also the One sent by God to heal spiritual affliction.

3. The Pharisees, who already hated Jesus, believed He had sinned by performing a miracle on the Sabbath day. Some seemed to realize that in the miracle God had acted in a way contrary to their belief of how God would act. Perhaps we face similar struggles with issues such as cloning, organ transplants, or certain scientific discoveries.

4. It seems the son was not as concerned with excommunication as were his parents. Certainly Jesus had made a great impact on him. Also, the man's blindness may already have caused him to be considered an outsider.

5. In love Jesus had given sight to the man, who realized that Jesus was from God. But Jesus wanted more. He wanted the man to have saving faith.

6. The purpose of Jesus' miracles was for Jesus to reveal Himself as the true Messiah. The man's confession of faith proves that Jesus fulfilled His purpose in this miracle.

Apply

Read aloud or invite volunteers to read aloud the paragraphs in this section. The "Apply" section will help participants apply the truths revealed in the scriptural account to their own lives. After reading the introductory section, answer the questions that follow.

1. Sin has consequences. The consequences of sin are visible throughout the world and include war, sickness, alcoholism, violence, and so forth. These consequences are a result of people's sinful behaviors. Even natural events—for example, earthquakes, tornadoes, and hurricanes—are a result of the fall into sin. Through the sin of Adam and Eve, violence, catastrophe, trouble, and hardships became a part of the world that God had created perfectly. To assume that a disease, trouble, or hardship is the result of a particular sin—the sin of parents, family, or oneself—is an erroneous, nonscriptural teaching.

2. Through afflictions God continues to work miracles. Often when people encounter troubles and hardships, they realize their helplessness. God can and will seize the opportunity to strengthen people's faith as they realize that only God can handle the troubles they encounter. Through His Word, God continues to strengthen the faith of believers, even as they face traumatic events.

3. Encourage participants to share passages that are meaningful to them in difficult situations. Consider role-playing a conversation with the youth.

4. Take time to discuss this issue. Blind people tend to be hidden from society and very much in need of support.

5. Answers will vary. We were born in darkness because of sin. At our Baptism, God called us out of darkness into the light of faith. Urge participants to share their analogies with others in the group.

6. We are lights to the world as we demonstrate our saving faith in the person and work of Jesus through our actions and our words. God uses us as His lights to bring light into the lives of people living in darkness.

Catechism Connection

1. The words of Isaiah 53:5 summarize the purpose of Christ's suffering and death—and of His entire ministry.

2. Answers will vary.

3. Isaiah 53 describes what Christ did for us. John 3:16 tells why He did it.

Send

To Do This Week

Urge participants to complete one or more of the "Family Connection" activities and one or more of the "For Personal Reflection" activities during the coming week. Then close with prayer.

For Next Week

Urge participants to read the assigned portion of Scripture in preparation for the next class session.